The Doors Of Perception

& Heaven and Hell

Aldous Huxley

This Edition Published by Thinking Ink 2011

Cover Design by Andrew Marshall

A CIP Catalogue for this book is available from the
British Library.

ISBN 978-1-907590-09-2

Thinking Ink Limited

LONDON   NEW YORK   SYDNEY

TABLE OF CONTENTS

Introduction

IN 1952 Aldous Huxley became involved in the now legendary experiment to clinically detail the physiological and psychological effects of the little known drug used by Mexican and Native American elders in religious practices. The drug was Peyote—now commonly know as mescalin.

By the standards of the time, Huxley was a hard working, respected, and reserved intellectual from a highly intelligent, well-know, and eccentric British family. By any standards, the results of the experiment were remarkable.

The Doors of Perception and *Heaven and Hell* detail the practicalities of the experiment and give Huxley's vivid account of his immediate experience and the more prolonged effect upon his subsequent thinking and awareness.

At first, the reader is drawn in by the sheer naivety and tomfoolery of the proposal but is soon caught in a finely woven net by the juxtaposition of Huxley's formidable intellect, his remarkable ability to convey the experience in such acute and truthful detail, and his incredible modesty.

In 1922 Gertrude Stein famously wrote - *A rose is a rose is a rose*. In proving her right, Huxley also shows the deeper meaning behind the apparently simple verse and goes on to deliver such spectacular accounts of the most everyday objects that the reason for their repeated and continual renderings by all the major artists throughout history suddenly becomes quite clear. For the conscious and willing reader - a trip to the Guggenheim, the Louvre or the Tate Modern will never be the same again.

Enjoy . . .

Robbie McCallum

i

THE DOORS OF PERCEPTION

I
T WAS IN 1886 that the German pharmacologist, Louis Lewin, published the first systematic study of the cactus, to which his own name was subsequently given. *Anhalonium lewinii* was new to science. To primitive religion and the Indians of Mexico and the American Southwest it was a friend of immemorially long standing. Indeed, it was much more than a friend. In the words of one of the early Spanish visitors to the New World, "they eat a root which they call peyote, and which they venerate as though it were a deity."

Why they should have venerated it as a deity became apparent when such eminent psychologists as Jaensch, Havelock Ellis and Weir Mitchell began their experiments with mescalin, the active principle of peyote.

True, they stopped short at a point well this side of idolatry; but all concurred in assigning to mescalin a position among drugs of unique distinction. Administered in suitable doses, it changes the quality of consciousness more profoundly and yet is less toxic than any other substance in the pharmacologist's repertory.

Mescalin research has been going on sporadically ever since the days of Lewin and Havelock Ellis. Chemists have not merely isolated the alkaloid; they have learned how to synthesize it, so that the supply no longer depends on the sparse and intermittent crop of a desert cactus. Alienists have dosed themselves with mescalin in the hope thereby of coming to abetter, a first-hand, understanding of their patients' mental processes.

Working unfortunately upon too few subjects within too narrow a range of circumstances, psychologists have observed and catalogued some of the drug's more striking effects. Neurologists and physiologists have found out something about the mechanism of its action upon the central nervous system. And at least one professional philosopher has taken mescalin for the light it may

1

throw on such ancient, unsolved riddles as the place of mind in nature and the relationship between brain and consciousness.

There matters rested until, two or three years ago, a new and perhaps highly significant fact was observed.* Actually the fact had been staring everyone in the face for several decades; but nobody, as it happened, had noticed it until a Young English psychiatrist, at present working in Canada, was struck by the close similarity, in chemical composition, between mescalin and adrenaline. Further research revealed that lysergic acid, an extremely potent hallucinogen derived from ergot, has a structural biochemical relationship to the others. Then came the discovery that adrenochrome, which is a product of the decomposition of adrenaline, can produce many of the symptoms observed in mescalin intoxication. Butadrenochrome probably occurs spontaneously in the human body. In other words, each one of us may be capable of manufacturing a chemical, minute doses of which are known to cause profound changes in consciousness. Certain of these changes are similar to those which occur in that most characteristic plague of the twentyeth century, schizophrenia.

Is the mental disorder due to a chemical disorder? And is the chemical disorder due, in its turn, to psychological distresses affecting the adrenals?

It would be rash and premature to affirm it. The most we can say is that some kind of a *prima facie* case has been made out. Meanwhile the clue is being systematically followed, the sleuths—biochemists, psychiatrists, psychologists—are on the trail.

By a series of, for me, extremely fortunate circumstances I found myself, in the spring of 1953, squarely athwart that trail. One of the sleuths had come on business to California. In spite of seventy years of mescalin research, the psychological material at his disposal was still absurdly inadequate, and he was anxious to add to it. I was on the spot and willing, indeed eager, to be a guinea pig. Thus it came about that, one bright May morning, I swallowed four-tenths of a gram of mescalin dissolved in half a glass of water and sat down to wait for the results.

We live together, we act on, and react to, one another; but always and in all circumstances we are by ourselves. The martyrs go hand in hand into the arena; they are crucified alone. Embraced, the lovers desperately try to fuse their insulated ecstasies into a single self-transcendence; in vain. By its very nature every embodied spirit is doomed to suffer and enjoy in solitude.

Sensations, feelings, insights, fancies—all these are private and, except through symbols and at second hand, incommunicable.

We can pool information about experiences, but never the experiences themselves. From family to nation, every human group is a society of island universes.

Most island universes are sufficiently like one another to permit of inferential understanding or even of mutual empathy or "feeling into."

Thus, remembering our own bereavements and humiliations, we can condole with others in analogous circumstances, can put our-selves (always, of course, in a slightly Pickwickian sense) in their places. But uncertain cases communication between universes is incomplete or even nonexistent. The mind is its own place, and the Places inhabited by the insane and the exceptionally gifted are so different from the places where ordinary men and women live, that there is little or no common ground of memory to serve as a basis for understanding or fellow feeling. Words are uttered, but fail to enlighten. The things and events to which the symbols refer belong to mutually exclusive realms of experience.

To see ourselves as others see us is a most salutary gift. Hardly less important is the capacity to see others as they see themselves. But what if these others belong to a different species and inhabit a radically alien universe? For example, how can the sane get to know what it actually feels like to be mad? Or, short of being born again as a visionary, a medium, or a musical genius, how can we ever visit the worlds which, to Blake, to Swedenborg, to Johann Sebastian Bach, were home? And how can a man at the extreme limits of ectomorphy and cerebrotonia ever put himself in the place of one at the limits of endomorphy and viscerotonia, or, except within certain circumscribed areas, share the feelings of one who stands at the limits of mesomorphy and somatotonia? To the unmitigated behaviourist such questions, I suppose, are meaningless. But for those who theoretically believe what in practice they know to be true—namely, that there is an inside to experience as well as an outside—the problems posed are real problems, all the more grave for being, some completely insoluble, some soluble only in exceptional circumstances and by methods not available to everyone. Thus, it seems virtually certain that I shall never know what it feels like to be Sir John Falstaff or Joe Louis. On the other hand, it had always seemed to me possible that, through hypnosis, for example, or auto-hypnosis, by means of systematic meditation, or else by taking the appropriate drug, I might so change my ordinary mode of consciousness as to be able to know, from the inside, what the visionary, the medium, even the mystic were talking about.

From what I had read of the mescalin experience I was convinced in advance that the drug would admit me, at least for a few hours, into the kind of inner world described by Blake and AE. But what I had expected did not happen. I had expected to lie with my eyes shut, looking at visions of many-coloured geometries, of animated architectures, rich with gems and fabulously lovely, of landscapes with heroic figures, of symbolic dramas trembling perpetually on the verge of the ultimate revelation. But I had not reckoned, it was evident, with the idiosyncrasies of my mental make-up, the facts of my temperament, training and habits.

I am and, for as long as I can remember, I have always been a poor visualizer. Words, even the pregnant words of poets, do not evoke pictures in my mind. No hypnagogic visions greet me on the verge of sleep.

When I recall something, the memory does not present itself to me as a vividly seen event or object. By an effort of the will, I can evoke a not very vivid image of what happened yesterday afternoon, of how the Lungarno used to look before the bridges were destroyed, of the Bayswater Road when the only buses were green and tiny and drawn by aged horses at three and a half miles an hour. But such images have little substance and absolutely no autonomous life of their own. They stand to real, perceived objects in the same relation as Homer's ghosts stood to the men of flesh and blood, who came to visit them in the shades. Only when I have a high temperature do my mental images come to independent life. To those in whom the faculty of visualization is strong my inner world must seem curiously drab, limited and uninteresting. This was the world—a poor thing but my own—which I expected to see transformed into something completely unlike itself.

The change which actually took place in that world was in no sense revolutionary. Half an hour after swallowing the drug I became aware of a slow dance of golden lights. A little later there were sumptuous red surfaces swelling and expanding from bright nodes of energy that vibrated with a continuously changing, patterned life. At another time the closing of my eyes revealed a complex of gray structures, within which pale bluish spheres kept emerging into intense solidity and, having emerged, would slide noiselessly upwards, out of sight. But at no time were there faces or forms of men or animals. I saw no landscapes, no enormous spaces, no magical growth and metamorphosis of buildings, nothing remotely like a drama or a parable. The other world to which mescalin admitted me was not the world of visions; it existed out there, in what I could see with my eyes open. The great change was in the realm of objective fact. What had happened to my subjective universe was relatively unimportant.

I took my pill at eleven. An hour and a half later, I was sitting in my study, looking intently at a small glass vase. The vase contained only three flowers—a full-blown Belie of Portugal rose, shell pink with a hint at every petal's base of a hotter, flamier hue; a large magenta and cream-colored carnation; and, pale purple at the end of its broken stalk, the bold heraldic blossom of an iris. Fortuitous and provisional, the little nosegay broke all the rules of traditional good taste. At breakfast that morning I had been struck by the lively dissonance of its colours. But that was no longer the point. I was not looking now at an unusual flower arrangement. I was seeing what Adam had seen on the morning of his creation—the miracle, moment by moment, of naked existence.

"Is it agreeable?" somebody asked. (During this part of the experiment, all conversations were recorded on a dictating machine, and it has been possible for me to refresh my memory of what was said.)

"Neither agreeable nor disagreeable," I answered. "It just is."

Istigkeit—wasn't that the word Meister Eckhart liked to use? "Is-ness." The Being of Platonic philosophy— except that Plato seems to have made the enormous, the grotesque mistake of separating Being from becoming and identifying it with the mathematical abstraction of the Idea. He could never, poor fellow, have seen a bunch of flowers shining with their own inner light and all but quivering under the pressure of the significance with which they were charged; could never have perceived that what rose and iris and carnation so intensely signified was nothing more, and nothing less, than what they were—a transience that was yet eternal life, a perpetual perishing that was at the same time pure Being, a bundle of minute, unique particulars in which, by some unspeakable and yet self-evident paradox, was to be seen the divine source of all existence.

I continued to look at the flowers, and in their living light I seemed to detect the qualitative equivalent of breathing—but of a breathing without returns to a starting point, with no recurrent ebbs but only a repeated flow from beauty to heightened beauty, from deeper to ever deeper meaning. Words like "grace" and "transfiguration" came to my mind, and this, of course, was what, among other things, they stood for. My eyes travelled from the rose to the carnation, and from that feathery incandescence to the smooth scrolls of sentient amethyst which were the iris. The Beatific Vision, Sat Chit Ananda, Being-Awareness-Bliss—for the first time I understood, not on the verbal level, not by inchoate hints or at a distance, but precisely and completely what those prodigious syllables referred to.

And then I remembered a passage I had read in one of Suzuki's essays.

"What is the Dharma-Body of the Buddha?" ('"the Dharma-Body of the Buddha" is another way of saying Mind, Suchness, the Void, the Godhead.) The question is asked in a Zen monastery by an earnest and bewildered novice. And with the prompt irrelevance of one of the Marx Brothers, the Master answers, "The hedge at the bottom of the garden." "And the man who realizes this truth," the novice dubiously inquires, "what, may I ask, is he?" Groucho gives him a whack over the shoulders with his staff and answers, "A golden-haired lion."

It had been, when I read it, only a vaguely pregnant piece of nonsense. Now it was all as clear as day, as evident as Euclid. Of course the Dharma-Body of the Buddha was the hedge at the bottom of the garden.

At the same time, and no less obviously, it was these flowers, it was anything that I—or rather the blessed Not-I, released for a moment from my throttling embrace—cared to look at. The books, for example, with which my study walls were lined. Like the flowers, they glowed, when I looked at them, with brighter colours, a pro-founder significance. Red books, like rubies; emerald books; books bound in white jade; books of agate; of aquamarine, of yellow topaz; lapis lazuli books whose colour was so intense, so intrinsically meaningful, that they seemed to be on the point of leaving the shelves to thrust themselves more insistently on my attention.

"What about spatial relationships?" the investigator inquired, as I was looking at the books.

It was difficult to answer. True, the perspective looked rather odd,

6

and the walls of the room no longer seemed to meet in right angles. But these were not the really important facts. The really important facts were that spatial relationships had ceased to matter very much and that my mind was perceiving the world in terms of other than spatial categories.

At ordinary times the eye concerns itself with such problems as Where?—How far?—How situated in relation to what? In the mescalin experience the implied questions to which the eye responds are of another order.

Place and distance cease to be of much interest. The mind does its Perceiving in terms of intensity of existence, profundity of significance, relationships within a pattern. I saw the books, but was not at all concerned with their positions in space. What I noticed, what impressed itself upon my mind was the fact that all of them glowed with living light and that in some the glory was more manifest than in others. In this context position and the three dimensions were beside the point. Not, of course, that the category of space had been abolished. When I got up and walked about, I could do so quite normally, without misjudging the whereabouts of objects. Space was still there; but it had lost its predominance. The mind was primarily concerned, not with measures and locations, but with being and meaning.

And along with indifference to space there went an even more complete indifference to time. "There seems to be plenty of it," was all I would answer, when the investigator asked me to say what I felt about time. Plenty of it, but exactly how much was entirely irrelevant. I could, of course, have looked at my watch; but my watch, I knew, was in another universe. My actual experience had been, was still, of an indefinite duration or alternatively of a perpetual present made up of one continually changing apocalypse.

From the books the investigator directed my attention to the furniture. A small typing table stood in the centre of the room; beyond it, from my point of view, was a wicker chair and beyond that a desk. The three pieces formed an intricate pattern of horizontals, uprights and diagonals—a pattern all the more interesting for not being interpreted in terms of spatial relationships. Table, chair and desk came together in a composition that was like something by Braque or Juan Gris, a still life recognizably related to the objective world, but rendered without depth, without any attempt at photographic realism. I was looking at my furniture, not as the utilitarian who has to sit on chairs, to write at desks and tables, and not as the cameraman or scientific recorder, but as the pure aesthete whose concern is only with forms and their relationships within the field of vision or the picture space. But as I looked, this purely aesthetic, Cubist's-eye view gave place to what I can only describe as the sacramental vision of reality. I was back where I had been when I was looking at the flowers—back in a world where everything shone with the Inner Light, and was infinite in its significance. The legs, for example, of that chair—how miraculous their tubularity, how supernatural their polished smoothness! I spent several minutes—or was it several centuries?—not merely gazing at those bamboo legs, but actually being them—or rather being myself in them; or, to be still more accurate (for "I" was not involved in the case, nor in a certain sense were "they") being my Not-self in the Not-self which was the chair.

Reflecting on my experience, I find myself agreeing with the eminent Cambridge philosopher, Dr. C. D. Broad, "that we should do well to consider much more seriously than we have hitherto been inclined to do the type of theory which Bergson put forward in connection with memory and sense perception. The suggestion is that the function of the brain and nervous system and sense organs is in the main eliminative and not productive. Each person is at each moment capable of remembering all that has ever happened to him and of perceiving everything that is happening everywhere in the universe. The function of the brain and nervous system is to protect us from being overwhelmed and confused by this mass of largely useless and irrelevant knowledge, by shutting out most of what we should otherwise perceive or remember at any moment, and leaving only that very small and special selection which is likely to be practically useful." According to such a theory, each one of us is potentially Mind at Large. But in so far as we are animals, our business is at all costs to survive. To make biological survival possible, Mind at Large has to be funnelled through the reducing valve of the brain and nervous system. What comes out at the other end is a measly trickle of the kind of consciousness which will help us to stay alive on the surface of this particular planet. To formulate and express the contents of this reduced awareness, man has invented and endlessly elaborated those symbol systems and implicit philosophies which we call languages. Every individual is at once the beneficiary and the victim of the linguistic tradition into which he has been born—the beneficiary inasmuch as language gives access to the accumulated records of other people's experience, the victim in so far as it confirms him in the belief that reduced awareness is the only awareness and as it bedevils his sense of reality, so that he is all too apt to take his concepts for data, his words for actual things. That which, in the language of religion, is called "this world" is the universe of reduced awareness, expressed, and, as it were, petrified by language. The various "other worlds," with which human beings erratically make contact are so many elements in the totality of the awareness belonging to Mind at Large. Most people, most of the time, know only what comes through the reducing valve and is consecrated as genuinely real by the local language. Certain persons, however, seem to be born with a kind of by-pass that circumvents the reducing valve. In others temporary bypasses may be acquired either spontaneously, or as the result of deliberate "spiritual exercises," or through hypnosis, or by means of drugs.

Through these permanent or temporary by-passes there flows, not indeed the perception "of everything that is happening everywhere in the universe" (for the by-pass does not abolish the reducing valve, which still excludes the total content of Mind at Large), but something more than, and above all something different from, the carefully selected utilitarian material which our narrowed, individual minds regard as a complete, or at least sufficient, picture of reality.

The brain is provided with a number of enzyme systems which serve to co-ordinate its workings. Some of these enzymes regulate the supply of glucose to the brain cells. Mescalin inhibits the production of these enzymes and thus lowers the amount of glucose available to an organ that is in constant need of sugar. When mescalin reduces the brain's normal ration of sugar what happens? Too few cases have been observed, and therefore a comprehensive answer cannot yet be given. But what happens to the majority of the few who have taken mescalin under supervision can be summarized as follows.

> (1) The ability to remember and to "think straight" is little if at all reduced. (Listening to the recordings of my conversation under the influence of the drug, I cannot discover that I was then any stupider than I am at ordinary times.)
> (2) Visual impressions are greatly intensified and the eye recovers some of the perceptual innocence of child-hood, when the sensum was not immediately and

automatically subordinated to the concept. Interest in space is diminished and interest in time falls almost to zero.

(3) Though the intellect remains unimpaired and though perception is enormously improved, the will suffers a profound change for the worse. The mescalin taker sees no reason for doing anything in particular and finds most of the causes for which, at ordinary times, he was prepared to act and suffer, profoundly uninteresting. He can't be bothered with them, for the good reason that he has better things to think about.

(4) These better things may be experienced (as I experienced them) "out there," or "in here," or in both worlds, the inner and the outer, simultaneously or successively. That they are better seems to be self-evident to all mescalin takers who come to the drug with a sound liver and an untroubled mind.

These effects of mescalin are the sorts of effects you could expect to follow the administration of a drug having the power to impair the efficiency of the cerebral reducing valve. When the brain runs out of sugar, the undernourished ego grows weak, can't be bothered to undertake the necessary chores, and loses all interest in those spatial and temporal relationships which mean so much to an organism bent on getting on in the world. As Mind at Large seeps past the no longer watertight valve, all kinds of biologically useless things start to happen. In some cases there may be extra-sensory perceptions. Other persons discover a world of visionary beauty. To others again is revealed the glory, the infinite value and meaningfulness of naked existence, of the given, unconceptualized event. In the final stage of egolessness there is an "obscure knowledge" that All is in all—that All is actually each. This is as near, I take it, as a finite mind can ever come to "perceiving everything that is happening everywhere in the universe."

In this context, how significant is the enormous heightening, under mescalin, of the perception of colour! For certain animals it is biologically very important to be able to distinguish certain hues. But beyond the limits of their utilitarian spectrum, most creatures are completely colour-blind. Bees, for example, spend most of their time "deflowering the fresh virgins of the spring"; but, as Von Frisch has shown, they can recognize only a very few colours. Man's highly developed colour sense is a biological luxury—

inestimably precious to him as an intellectual and spiritual being, but unnecessary to his survival as an animal. To judge by the adjectives which Homer puts into their mouths, the heroes of the Trojan War hardly excelled the bees in their capacity to distinguish colours. In this respect, at least, mankind's advance has been prodigious.

Mescalin raises all colours to a higher power and makes the percipient aware of innumerable fine shades of difference, to which, at ordinary times, he is completely blind. It would seem that, for Mind at Large, the so-called secondary characters of things are primary. Unlike Locke, it evidently feels that colours are more important, better worth attending to, than masses, positions and dimensions. Like mescalin takers, many mystics perceive super-naturally brilliant colours, not only with the inward eye, but even in the objective world around them. Psychics and sensitives make similar reports. There are certain mediums to whom the mescalin taker's brief revelation is a matter, during long periods, of daily and hourly experience.

From this long but indispensable excursion into the realm of theory, we may now return to the miraculous facts—four bamboo chair legs in the middle of a room. Like Wordsworth's daffodils, they brought all manner of wealth—the gift, beyond price, of a new direct insight into the very Nature of Things, together with a more modest treasure of understanding in the field, especially, of the arts.

A rose is a rose is a rose. But these chair legs were chair legs were St. Michael and all angels. Four or five hours after the event, when the effects of a cerebral sugar shortage were wearing off, I was taken for a little tour of the city, which included a visit, towards sundown, to what is modestly claimed to be the World's Biggest Drug Store. At the back of the W.B.D.S., among the toys, the greeting cards and the comics, stood a row, surprisingly enough, of art books. I picked up the first volume that came to hand. It was on Van Gogh, and the picture at which the book opened was "The Chair"—that astounding portrait of a *Ding an Sich*, which the mad painter saw, with a kind of adoring terror, and tried to render on his canvas. But it was a task to which the power even of genius proved wholly inadequate. The chair Van Gogh had seen was obviously the same in essence as the chair I had seen. But, though incomparably more real than the chairs of ordinary perception, the chair in his picture remained no more than an

11

unusually expressive symbol of the fact. The fact had been manifested Suchness; this was only an emblem. Such emblems are sources of true knowledge about the Nature of Things, and this true knowledge may serve to prepare the mind which accepts it for immediate insights on its own account. But that is all. However expressive, symbols can never be the things they stand for.

It would be interesting, in this context, to make a study of the works of art available to the great knowers of Suchness. What sort of pictures did Eckhart look at? What sculptures and paintings played a part in the religious experience of St. John of the Cross, of Hakuin, of Hui-neng, of William Law? The questions are beyond my power to answer; but I strongly suspect that most of the great knowers of Suchness paid very little attention to art—some refusing to have anything to do with it at all, others being content with what a critical eye would regard as second-rate, or even, tenth-rate, works. (To a person whose transfigured and trans-figuring mind can see the All in every this, the first-rateness or tenth-rateness of even a religious painting will be a matter of the most sovereign indifference.) Art, I suppose, is only for beginners, or else for those resolute dead-enders, who have made up their minds to be content with the ersatz of Suchness, with symbols rather than with what they signify, with the elegantly composed recipe in lieu of actual dinner.

I returned the Van Gogh to its rack and picked up the volume standing next to it. It was a book on Botticelli. I turned the pages. "The Birth of Venus"—never one of my favourites. "Mars and Venus," that loveliness so passionately denounced by poor Ruskin at the height of his long-drawn sexual tragedy. The marvellously rich and intricate "Calumny of Apelles." And then a somewhat less familiar and not very good picture, "Judith." My attention was arrested and I gazed in fascination, not at the pale neurotic heroine or her attendant, not at the victim's hairy head or the vernal landscape in the background, but at the purplish silk of Judith's pleated bodice and long wind-blown skirts.

This was something I had seen before—seen that very morning, between the flowers and the furniture, when I looked down by chance, and went on passionately staring by choice, at my own crossed legs. Those folds in the trousers—what a labyrinth of endlessly significant complexity! And the texture of the gray flannel—how rich, how deeply, mysteriously sumptuous! And here they were again, in Botticelli's picture.

Civilized human beings wear clothes, therefore there can be no portraiture, no mythological or historical storytelling without representations of folded textiles. But though it may account for the origins, mere tailoring can never explain the luxuriant development of drapery as a major theme of all the plastic arts. Artists, it is obvious, have always loved drapery for its own sake—or, rather, for their own. When you paint or carve drapery, you are painting or carving forms which, for all practical purposes, are non-representational—the kind of unconditioned forms on which artists even in the most naturalistic tradition like to let themselves go. In the average Madonna or Apostle the strictly human, fully representational element accounts for about ten per cent of the whole. All the rest consists of many coloured variations on the inexhaustible theme of crumpled wool or linen. And these nonrepresentational nine-tenths of a Madonna or an Apostle may be just as important qualitatively as they are in quantity. Very often they set the tone of the whole work of art, they state the key in which the theme is being rendered, they express the mood, the temperament, the attitude to life of the artist. Stoical serenity reveals itself in the smooth surfaces, the broad untortured folds of Piero's draperies. Torn between fact and wish, between cynicism and idealism, Bernini tempers the all but caricatural verisimilitude of his faces with enormous sartorial abstractions, which are the embodiment, in stone or bronze, of the everlasting commonplaces of rhetoric—the heroism, the holiness, the sublimity to which mankind perpetually aspires, for the most part in vain. And here are El Greco's disquietingly visceral skirts and mantles; here are the sharp, twisting, flame-like folds in which Cosimo Tura clothes his figures: in the first, traditional spirituality breaks down into a nameless physiological yearning; in the second, there writhes an agonized sense of the world's essential strangeness and hostility. Or consider Watteau; his men and women play lutes, get ready for balls and harlequinades, embark, on velvet lawns and under noble trees, for the Cythera of every lover's dream; their enormous melancholy and the flayed, excruciating sensibility of their creator find expression, not in the actions recorded, not in the gestures and the faces portrayed, but in the relief and texture of their taffeta skirts, their satin capes and doublets. Not an inch of smooth surface here, not a moment of peace or confidence, only a silken wilderness of countless tiny pleats and wrinkles, with an incessant modulation—inner uncertainty rendered with the perfect assurance of a master hand—of tone into tone, of one indeterminate colour into another. In life, man proposes, God disposes. In the plastic arts the proposing is done by the subject matter; that which disposes is ultimately the artist's temperament, proximately (at least in portraiture, history and genre) the carved or painted drapery. Between them, these two may decree that a *fête galante* shall move to tears, that a crucifixion shall be serene to the point of cheerfulness, that a stigmatization shall be almost intolerably sexy, that the likeness of a prodigy of female brainlessness (I am thinking now of Ingres' incomparable Mme. Moitessier) shall express the austerest, the most uncompromising intellectuality.

But this is not the whole story. Draperies, as I had now discovered, are much more than devices for the introduction of non-representational forms into naturalistic paintings and sculptures. What the rest of us see only under the influence of mescalin, the artist is congenitally equipped to see all the time. His perception is not limited to what is biologically or socially useful. A little of the knowledge belonging to Mind at Large oozes past the reducing valve of brain and ego, into his consciousness. It is a knowledge of the intrinsic significance of every existent. For the artist as for the mescalin taker draperies are living hieroglyphs that stand in some peculiarly expressive way for the unfathomable mystery of pure being.

More even than the chair, though less perhaps than those wholly supernatural flowers, the folds of my gray flannel trousers were charged with "is-ness." To what they owed this privileged status, I cannot say. Is it, perhaps, because the forms of folded drapery are so strange and dramatic that they catch the eye and in this way force the miraculous fact of sheer existence upon the attention? Who knows? What is important is less the reason for the experience than the experience itself. Poring over Judith's skirts, there in the World's Biggest Drug Store, I knew that Botticelli—and not Botticelli alone, but many others too—had looked at draperies with the same transfigured and transfiguring eyes as had been mine that morning. They had seen the Istigkeit, the Allness and Infinity of folded cloth and had done their best to render it in paint or stone. Necessarily, of course, without success. For the glory and the wonder of pure existence belong to another order, beyond the Power of even the highest art to express. But in Judith's skirt I could clearly see what, if I had been a painter of genius, I might have made of my old gray flannels. Not much, heaven knows, in

14

comparison with the reality, but enough to delight generation after generation of beholders, enough to make them understand at least a little of the true significance of what, in our pathetic imbecility, we call "mere things" and disregard in favour of television.

"This is how one ought to see," I kept saying as I looked down at my trousers, or glanced at the jewelled books in the shelves, at the legs of my infinitely more than Van-Goghian chair. "This is how one ought to see, how things really are." And yet there were reservations. For if one always saw like this, one would never want to do anything else. Just looking, just being the divine Not-self of flower, of book, of chair, of flannel. That would be enough. But in that case what about other people? What about human relations? In the recording of that morning's conversations I find the question constantly repeated, "What about human relations?" How could one reconcile this timeless bliss of seeing as one ought to see with the temporal duties of doing what one ought to do and feeling as one ought to feel? "One ought to be able," I said, "to see these trousers as infinitely important and human beings as still more infinitely important."

One ought—but in practice it seemed to be impossible. This participation in the manifest glory of things left no room, so to speak, for the ordinary, the necessary concerns of human existence, above all for concerns involving persons. For Persons are selves and, in one respect at least, I was now a Not-self, simultaneously perceiving and being the Not-self of the things around me. To this new-born Not-self, the behaviour, the appearance, the very thought of the self it had momentarily ceased to be, and of other selves, its one-time fellows, seemed not indeed distasteful (for distastefulness was not one of the categories in terms of which I was thinking), but enormously irrelevant. Compelled by the investigator to analyze and report on what I was doing (and how I longed to be left alone with Eternity in a flower, Infinity in four chair legs and the Absolute in the folds of a pair of flannel trousers!), I realized that I was deliberately avoiding the eyes of those who were with me in the room, deliberately refraining from being too much aware of them. One was my wife, the other a man I respected and greatly liked; but both belonged to the world from which, for the moment, mescalin had delivered me the world of selves, of time, of moral judgments and utilitarian considerations, the world (and it was this aspect of human life which I wished, above all else, to forget) of

15

self-assertion, of cocksureness, of overvalued words and idol-
atrously worshipped notions.

At this stage of the proceedings I was handed a large coloured
reproduction of the well-known self-portrait by Cézanne—the head
and shoulders of a man in a large straw hat, red-cheeked, red-
lipped, with rich black whiskers and a dark unfriendly eye. It is a
magnificent painting; but it was not as a painting that I now saw it.
For the head promptly took on a third dimension and came to life
as a small goblin-like man looking out through a window in the
page before me. I started to laugh. And when they asked me why,
"What pretensions!" I kept repeating. "Who on earth does he think
he is?" The question was not addressed to Cézanne in particular,
but to the human species at large. Who did they all think they
were?

"It's like Arnold Bennett in the Dolomites," I said, suddenly remembering a scene, happily immortalized in a snapshot, of A.B.,
some four or five years before his death, toddling along a wintry
road at Cortina d'Ampezzo. Around him lay the virgin snow; in
the background was a more than gothic aspiration of red crags.
And there was dear, kind, unhappy A.B., consciously overacting
the role of his favourite character in fiction, himself, the Card in
person. There he went, toddling slowly in the bright Alpine sunshine, his thumbs in the armholes of a yellow waistcoat which
bulged, a little lower down, with the graceful curve of a Regency
bow window at Brighton—his head thrown back as though to aim
some stammered utterance, howitzer-like, at the blue dome of
heaven. What he actually said, I have forgotten; but what his whole
manner, air and posture fairly shouted was, "I'm as good as those
damned mountains."

And in some ways, of course, he was infinitely better; but not,
as he knew very well, in the way his favourite character in fiction
liked to imagine.

Successfully (whatever that may mean) or unsuccessfully, we all
overact the part of our favourite character in fiction. And the fact,
the almost infinitely unlikely fact, of actually being Cézanne makes
no difference.

For the consummate painter, with his little pipeline to Mind at
Large bypassing the brain valve and ego-filter, was also and just as
genuinely this whiskered goblin with the unfriendly eye. For relief
I turned back to the folds in my trousers. "This is how one ought to
see," I repeated yet again. And I might have added, "These are the

16

sort of things one ought to look at." Things without pretensions, satisfied to be merely themselves, sufficient in their Suchness, not acting apart, not trying, insanely, to go it alone, in isolation from the Dharma Body, in Luciferian defiance of the grace of god.

"The nearest approach to this," I said, "would be a Vermeer."

Yes, a Vermeer. For that mysterious artist was truly gifted—with the vision that perceives the Dharma-Body as the hedge at the bottom of the garden, with the talent to render as much of that vision as the limitations of human capacity permit, and with the prudence to confine himself in his paintings to the more manageable aspects of reality; for though Vermeer represented human beings, he was always a painter of still life.

Cézanne, who told his female sitters to do their best to look like apples, tried to paint portraits in the same spirit. But his pippin-like women are more nearly related to Plato's Ideas than to the Dharma-Body in the hedge.

They are Eternity and Infinity seen, not in sand or flower, but in the abstractions of some very superior brand of geometry. Vermeer never asked his girls to look like apples. On the contrary, he insisted on their being girls to the very limit—but always with the proviso that they refrain from behaving girlishly. They might sit or quietly stand but never giggle, never display self-consciousness, never say their prayers or pine for absent sweethearts, never gossip, never gaze enviously at other women's babies, never dirt, never love or hate or work. In the act of doing any of these things they would doubtless become more intensely themselves, but would cease, for that very reason, to manifest their divine essential Not self. In Blake's phrase, the doors of Vermeer's perception were only partially cleansed. A single panel had become almost perfectly transparent; the rest of the door was still muddy. The essential Not-self could be perceived very clearly in things and in living creatures on the hither side of good and evil. In human beings it was visible only when they were in repose, their minds untroubled, their bodies motionless. In these circumstances Vermeer could see Suchness in all its heavenly beauty—could see and, in some small measure, render it—in a subtle and sumptuous still life. Vermeer is undoubtedly the greatest painter of human still lives. But there have been others, for example, Vermeer's French contemporaries, the Le Nain brothers. They set out, I suppose, to be genre painters; but what they actually produced was a series of human still lives, in which their cleansed perception of the infinite significance of all things is rendered not, as with Vermeer, by subtle enrichment of colour and texture, but by a heightened clarity, an obsessive distinctness of form, within an austere, almost monochromatic tonality. In our own day we have had Vuillard, the painter, at his best, of unforgettably splendid pictures of the Dharma-Body manifested in a bourgeois bedroom, of the absolute blazing away in the midst of some stockbroker's family in a suburban garden, taking tea.

> *Ce qui fait queue l'ancien bandagiste renie*
> *Le compote dont le faste alléchait les passants,*
> *C'est son jardin d'Auteuil, où, veufs de tout encens,*
> *Les Zinnias ont l'air d'être en tôle venire.*

For Laurent Taillade the spectacle was merely obscene. But if the retired rubber goods merchant had sat still enough, Vuillard would have seen in him only the Dharma-Body, would have painted, in the zinnias, the goldfish pool, the villa's Moorish tower and Chinese lanterns, a corner of Eden before the Fall.

But meanwhile my question remained unanswered. How was this cleansed perception to be reconciled with a proper concern with human relations, with the necessary chores and duties, to say nothing of charity and practical compassion? The age-old debate between the actives and the contemplatives was being renewed— renewed, so far as I was concerned, with an unprecedented poignancy. For until this morning I had known contemplation only in its humbler, its more ordinary forms—as discursive thinking; as a rapt absorption in poetry or painting or music; as a patient waiting upon those inspirations, without which even the prosiest writer cannot hope to accomplish anything; as occasional glimpses, in Nature, of Wordsworth's "something far more deeply inter-fused"; as systematic silence leading, sometimes, to hints of an "obscure knowledge." But now I knew contemplation at its height. At its height, but not yet in its fullness. For in its fullness the way of Mary includes the way of Martha and raises it, so to speak, to its own higher power. Mescalin opens up the way of Mary, but shuts the door on that of Martha. It gives access to contemplation—but to a contemplation that is incompatible with action and even with the will to action, the very thought of action. In the intervals between his revelations the mescalin taker is apt to feel that, though in one way everything is supremely as it should be, in another there is something wrong. His problem is essentially the same as that which confronts the quietist, the *arhat* and, on another level, the landscape painter and the painter of human still lives. Mescalin can never solve that problem; it can only pose it, apocalyptically, for those to whom it had never before presented itself. The full and final solution can be found only by those who are prepared to implement the right kind of Weltanschauung by means of the right kind of behaviour and the right kind of constant and unstrained alertness. Over against the quietist stands the active-contemplative, the saint, the man who, in Eckhart's phrase, is ready to come down from the seventh heaven in order to bring a cup of water to his sick brother. Over against the *arhat*, retreating from appearances into an entirely transcendental Nirvana, stands the Bodhisattva, for whom Suchness and the world of contingencies are one, and for whose boundless compassion every one of those contingencies is an occasion not only for transfiguring insight, but also for the most practical charity. And in the universe of art, over against Vermeer and the other Painters of human still lives, over against the masters of Chinese and Japanese landscape painting, over against Constable and Turner, against Sisley and Seurat and Cézanne, stands the all-inclusive art of Rembrandt. These are enormous names, inaccessible eminences. For myself, on this memorable May morning, I could only be grateful for an experience which had shown me, more clearly than I had ever seen it before, the true nature of the challenge and the completely liberating response.

Let me add, before we leave this subject, that there is no form of contemplation, even the most quietist, which is without its ethical values. Half at least of all morality is negative and consists in keeping out of mischief. The Lord's Prayer is less than fifty words long, and six of those words are devoted to asking God not to lead us into temptation. The one-sided contemplative leaves undone many things that he ought to do; but to make up for it, he refrains from doing a host of things he ought not to do. The sum of evil, Pascal remarked, would be much diminished if men could only learn to sit quietly in their rooms. The contemplative whose perception has been cleansed does not have to stay in his room. He can go about his business, so completely satisfied to see and be a part of the divine Order of Things that he will never even be tempted to indulge in what Traherne called "the dirty Devices of the world." When we feel ourselves to be sole heirs of the universe, when "the sea flows in our veins... and the stars are our jewels," when all things are perceived as infinite and holy, what motive can we have for covetousness or self-assertion, for the pursuit of power or the drearier forms of pleasure? Contemplatives are not likely to become gamblers, or procurers, or drunkards; they do not as a rule preach intolerance, or make war; do not find it necessary to rob, swindle or grind the faces of the poor. And to these enormous negative virtues we may add another which, though hard to define, is both positive and important. The *arhat* and the quietist may not practice contemplation in its fullness; but if they practice it at all, they may bring back enlightening reports of another, a transcendent country of the mind; and if they practice it in the height, they will become conduits through which some beneficent influence can flow out of that other country into a world of darkened selves, chronically dying for lack of it.

Meanwhile I had turned, at the investigator's request, from the portrait of Cézanne to what was going on, inside my head, when I shut my eyes. This time, the inscape was curiously unrewarding. The field of vision was filled with brightly coloured, constantly changing structures that seemed to be made of plastic or enamelled tin.

"Cheap," I commented. "Trivial. Like things in a five-and-ten." And all this shoddiness existed in a closed, cramped universe. "It's as though one were below decks in a ship," I said. "A five-and-ten-cent ship." And as I looked, it became very clear that this five-and-ten-cent ship was in some way connected with human pretensions, with the portrait of Cézanne, with A.B. among the Dolomites over-acting his favourite character in fiction. This suffocating interior of a dime-store ship was my own personal self; these gimcrack mobiles of tin and plastic were my personal contributions to the universe. I felt the lesson to be salutary, but was sorry, none the less, that it had had to be administered at this moment and in this form. As a rule the mescalin taker discovers an inner world as manifestly a datum, as self evidently "infinite and holy," as that transfigured outer world which I had seen with my eyes open. From the first, my own case had been different.

Mescalin had endowed me temporarily with the power to see things with my eyes shut; but it could not, or at least on this occasion did not, reveal an inscape remotely comparable to my flowers or chair or flannels "out there." What it had allowed me to perceive inside was not the Dharma Body, in images, but my own

20

mind; not Suchness, but a set of symbols—in other words, a homemade substitute for Suchness.

Most visualizers are transformed by mescalin into visionaries. Some of them—and they are Perhaps more numerous than is generally supposed—require no transformation; they are visionaries all the time. The mental species to which Blake belonged is fairly widely distributed even in the urban-industrial societies of the present day. The poet-artist's uniqueness does not consist in the fact that (to quote from his Descriptive Catalogue) he actually saw "those wonderful originals called in the Sacred Scriptures the Cherubim." It does not consist in the fact that "these wonderful originals seen in my visions, were some of them one hundred feet in height ... all containing mythological and recondite meaning." It consists solely in his ability to render, in words or (somewhat less successfully) in line and colour, some hint at least of a not excessively uncommon experience. The untalented visionary may perceive an inner reality no less tremendous, beautiful and significant than the world beheld by Blake; but he lacks altogether the ability to express, in literary or plastic symbols, what he has seen.

From the records of religion and the surviving monuments of poetry and the plastic arts it is very plain that, at most times and in most places, men have attached more importance to the inscape than to objective existents, have felt that what they saw with their eyes shut possessed a spiritually higher significance than what they saw with their eyes open. The reason? Familiarity breeds contempt, and how to survive is a problem ranging in urgency from the chronically tedious to the excruciating.

The outer world is what we wake up to every morning of our lives, is the place where, willy-nilly, we must try to make our living. In the inner world there is neither work nor monotony. We visit it only in dreams and musings, and its strangeness is such that we never find the same world on two successive occasions. What wonder, then, if human beings in their search for the divine have generally preferred to look within! Generally, but not always. In their art no less than in their religion, the Taoists and the Zen Buddhists looked beyond visions to the Void, and through the Void at "the ten thousand things" of objective reality. Because of their doctrine of the Word made flesh, Christians should have been able, from the first, to adopt a similar attitude towards the universe around them.

21

But because of the doctrine of the Fall, they found it very hard to do so. As recently as three hundred years ago an expression of thoroughgoing world denial and even world condemnation was both orthodox and comprehensible. "We should feel wonder at nothing at all in Nature except only the Incarnation of Christ." In the seventeenth century, Lallemant's phrase seemed to make sense. Today it has the ring of madness.

In China the rise of landscape painting to the rank of a major art form took place about a thousand, in Japan about six hundred and in Europe about three hundred, years ago. The equation of Dharma-Body with hedge was made by those Zen Masters, who wedded Taoist naturalism with Buddhist transcendentalism. It was, therefore, only in the Far East that landscape painters consciously regarded their art as religious. In the West religious painting was a matter of portraying sacred personages, of illustrating hallowed texts. Landscape painters regarded themselves as secularists. Today we recognize in Seurat one of the supreme masters of what may be called mystical landscape painting. And yet this man who was able, more effectively than any other, to render the One in the many, became quite indignant when somebody praised him for the "poetry" of his work. "I merely apply the System," he protested. In other words he was merely a pointilliste and, in his own eyes, nothing else. A similar anecdote is told of John Constable. One day towards the end of his life, Blake met Constable at Hampstead and was shown one of the younger artist's sketches. In spite of his contempt for naturalistic art, the old visionary knew a good thing when be saw it—except of course, when it was by Rubens. "This is not drawing," he cried, "this is inspiration!" "I had meant it to be drawing," was Constable's characteristic answer. Both men were right. It was drawing, precise and veracious, and at the same time it was inspiration—inspiration of an order at least as high as Blake's. The pine trees on the Heath had actually been seen as identical with the Dharma Body. The sketch was a rendering, necessarily imperfect but still profoundly impressive, of what a cleansed perception had revealed to the open eyes of a great painter. From a contemplation, in the tradition of Wordsworth and Whitman, of the Dharma-Body as hedge, and from visions, such as Blake's, of the "wonderful originals" within the mind, contemporary poets have retreated into an investigation of the personal, as opposed to the more than personal, subconscious and to a rendering, in highly abstract terms, not of the given, objective fact, but of mere scientific and theological notions. And something similar has happened in the field of painting, where we have witnessed a general retreat from landscape, the predominant art form of the nineteenth century. This retreat from landscape has not been into that other, inner divine Datum, with which most of the traditional schools of the past were concerned, that Archetypal World, where men have always found the raw materials of myth and religion. No, it has been a retreat from the outward Datum into the personal subconscious, into a mental world more squalid and more tightly closed than even the world of conscious personality. These contraptions of tin and highly coloured plastic—where had I seen them before? In every picture gallery that exhibits the latest in non-representational art.

And now someone produced a phonograph and put a record on the turntable. I listened with pleasure, but experienced nothing comparable to my seen apocalypses of flowers or flannel. Would a naturally gifted musician hear the revelations which, for me, had been exclusively visual?

It would be interesting to make the experiment. Meanwhile, though not transfigured, though retaining its normal quality and intensity, the music contributed not a little to my understanding of what had happened to me and of the wider problems which those happenings had raised.

Instrumental music, oddly enough, left me rather cold. Mozart's C Minor Piano Concerto was interrupted after the first movement, and a recording of some madrigals by Gesualdo took its place.

"These voices," I said appreciatively, "these voices—they're a kind of bridge back to the human world."

And a bridge they remained even while singing the most startlingly chromatic of the mad prince's compositions. Through the uneven phrases of the madrigals, the music pursued its course, never sticking to the same key for two bars together. In Gesualdo, that fantastic character out of a Webster melodrama, psychological disintegration had exaggerated, had pushed to the extreme limit, a tendency inherent in modal as opposed to fully tonal music. The resulting works sounded as though they might have been written by the later Schoenberg.

"And yet," I felt myself constrained to say, as I listened to these strange products of a Counter-Reformation psychosis working upon a late medieval art form, "and yet it does not matter that he's all in bits. The whole is disorganized. But each individual fragment

23

is in order, is a representative of a Higher Order. The Highest Order prevails even in the disintegration. The totality is present even in the broken pieces. More clearly present, perhaps, than in a completely coherent work. At least you aren't lulled into a sense of false security by some merely human, merely fabricated order. You have to rely on your immediate perception of the ultimate order. So in a certain sense disintegration may have its advantages. But of course it's dangerous, horribly dangerous. Suppose you couldn't get back, out of the chaos..."

From Gesualdo's madrigals we jumped, across a gulf of three centuries, to Alban Berg and the Lyric Suite.

"This," I announced in advance, "is going to be hell."

But, as it turned out, I was wrong. Actually the music sounded rather funny. Dredged up from the personal subconscious, agony succeeded twelve-tone agony; but what struck me was only the essential incongruity between a psychological disintegration even completer than Gesualdo's and the prodigious resources, in talent and technique, employed in its expression.

"Isn't he sorry for himself!" I commented with a derisive lack of sympathy. And then, "Katzenmusik—learned Katzenmusik." And finally, after a few more minutes of the anguish, "Who cares what his feelings are?

Why can't he pay attention to something else?"

As a criticism of what is undoubtedly a very remarkable work, it was unfair and inadequate—but not, I think, irrelevant. I cite it for what it is worth and because that is how, in a state of pure contemplation, I reacted to the Lyric Suite.

When it was over, the investigator suggested a walk in the garden. I was willing; and though my body seemed to have dissociated itself almost completely from my mind—or, to be more accurate, though my awareness of the transfigured outer world was no longer accompanied by an awareness of my physical organism—I found myself able to get up, open the French window and walk out with only a minimum of hesitation. It was odd, of course, to feel that "I" was not the same as these arms and legs "out there," as this wholly objective trunk and neck and even head. It was odd; but one soon got used to it. And anyhow the body seemed perfectly well able to look after itself. In reality, of course, it always does look after itself. All that the conscious ego can do is to formulate wishes, which are then carried out by forces which it controls very little and understands not at all. When it does anything more—when it tries too hard, for example, when it worries, when it becomes apprehensive about the future—it lowers the effectiveness of those forces and may even cause the devitalized body to fall ill. In my present state, awareness was not referred to as ego; it was, so to speak, on its own. This meant that the physiological intelligence controlling the body was also on its own. For the moment that interfering neurotic who, in waking hours, tries to run the show, was blessedly out of the way.

From the French window I walked out under a kind of pergola covered in part by a climbing rose tree, in part by laths, one inch wide with half an inch of space between them. The sun was shining and the shadows of the laths made a zebra-like pattern on the ground and across the seat and back of a garden chair, which was standing at this end of the pergola. That chair—shall I ever forget it? Where the shadows fell on the canvas upholstery, stripes of a deep but glowing indigo alternated with stripes of an incandescence so intensely bright that it was hard to believe that they could be made of anything but blue fire. For what seemed an immensely long time I gazed without knowing, even without wishing to know, what it was that confronted me. At any other time I would have seen a chair barred with alternate light and shade. Today the percept had swallowed up the concept. I was so completely absorbed in looking, so thunderstruck by what I actually saw, that I could not be aware of anything else. Garden furniture, laths, sunlight, shadow—these were no more than names and notions, mere verbalizations, for utilitarian or scientific purposes, after the event. The event was this succession of azure furnace doors separated by gulfs of unfathomable gentian. It was inexpressibly wonderful, wonderful to the point, almost, of being terrifying. And suddenly I had an inkling of what it must feel like to be mad. Schizophrenia has its heavens as well as its hells and purgatories.

I remember what an old friend, dead these many years, told me about his mad wife. One day in the early stages of the disease, when she still had her lucid intervals he had gone to talk to her about their children. She listened for a time, then cut him short. How could he bear to waste his time on a couple of absent children, when all that really mattered, here and now, was the unspeakable beauty of the patterns he made, in this brown tweed jacket, every time he moved his arms? Alas, this Paradise of cleansed perception, of pure one-sided contemplation, was not to endure. The blissful intermissions became rarer, became briefer, until finally there were no more of them; there was only horror.

Most takers of mescalin experience only the heavenly part of schizophrenia. The drug brings hell and purgatory only to those who have had a recent case of jaundice, or who suffer from periodical depressions or a chronic anxiety. If, like the other drugs of remotely comparable power, mescalin were notoriously toxic, the taking of it would be enough, of itself, to cause anxiety. But the reasonably healthy person knows in advance that, so far as he is concerned, mescalin is completely innocuous, that its effects will pass off after eight or ten hours, leaving no hangover and consequently no craving for a renewal of the dose. Fortified by this knowledge, he embarks upon the experiment without fear—in other words, without any disposition to convert an unprecedentedly strange and other than human experience into something appalling, something actually diabolical.

Confronted by a chair which looked like the Last Judgment—or, to be more accurate, by a Last Judgment which, after a long time and with considerable difficulty, I recognized as a chair—I found myself all at once on the brink of panic. This, I suddenly felt, was going too far. Too far, even though the going was into intenser beauty, deeper significance. The fear, as I analyze it in retrospect, was of being overwhelmed, of disintegrating under a pressure of reality greater than a mind accustomed to living most of the time in a cosy world of symbols could possibly bear. The literature of religious experience abounds in references to the pains and terrors overwhelming those who have come, too suddenly, face to face with some manifestation of the Mysterium tremendum. In theological language, this fear is due to the incompatibility between man's egotism and the divine purity, between man's self-aggravated separateness and the infinity of God. Following Boehme and William Law, we may say that, by unregenerate souls, the divine Light at its full blaze can be apprehended only as a burning, purgatorial fire.

An almost identical doctrine is to be found in The Tibetan Book of the Dead, where the departed soul is described as shrinking in agony from the Pure Light of the Void, and even from the lesser, tempered Lights, in order to rush headlong into the comforting darkness of selfhood as a reborn human being, or even as a beast, an unhappy ghost, a denizen of hell. Anything rather than the burning brightness of unmitigated Reality—anything!

The schizophrenic is a soul not merely unregenerate, but desperately sick into the bargain. His sickness consists in the inability to take refuge from inner and outer reality (as the sane person habitually does) in the homemade universe of common sense—the strictly human world of useful notions, shared symbols and socially acceptable conventions. The schizophrenic is like a man permanently under the influence of mescalin, and therefore unable to shut off the experience of a reality which he is not holy enough to live with, which he cannot explain away because it is the most stubborn of primary facts, and which, because it never permits him to look at the world with merely human eyes, scares him into interpreting its unremitting strangeness, its burning intensity of significance, as the manifestations of human or even cosmic malevolence, calling for the most desperate countermeasures, from murderous violence at one end of the scale to catatonia, or psychological suicide, at the other. And once embarked upon the downward, the infernal road, one would never be able to stop. That, now, was only too obvious.

"If you started in the wrong way," I said in answer to the investigator's questions, "everything that happened would be a proof of the conspiracy against you. It would all be self-validating. You couldn't draw a breath without knowing it was part of the plot."

"So you think you know where madness lies?"

My answer was a convinced and heartfelt, "Yes."

"And you couldn't control it?"

"No I couldn't control it. If one began with fear and hate as the major premise, one would have to go on to the conclusion."

"Would you be able," my wife asked, "to fix your attention on what The Tibetan Book of The Dead calls the Clear Light?"

I was doubtful.

"Would it keep the evil away, if you could hold it? Or would you not be able to hold it?"

I considered the question for some time. "Perhaps," I answered at last, "perhaps I could—but only if there were somebody there to tell me about the Clear Light. One couldn't do it by oneself. That's the point, I suppose, of the Tibetan ritual—someone sitting there all the time and telling you what's what."

After listening to the record of this part of the experiment, I took down my copy of Evans-Wentz's edition of The Tibetan Book of the Dead, and opened at random. "O nobly born, let not thy mind

27

be distracted." That was the problem—to remain undistracted. Undistracted by the memory of past sins, by imagined pleasure, by the bitter aftertaste of old wrongs and humiliations, by all the fears and hates and cravings that ordinarily eclipse the Light. What those Buddhist monks did for the dying and the dead, might not the modern psychiatrist do for the insane? Let there be a voice to assure them, by day and even while they are asleep, that in spite of all the terror, all the bewilderment and confusion, the ultimate Reality remains unshakably itself and is of the same substance as the inner light of even the most cruelly tormented mind. By means of such devices as recorders, clock-controlled switches, public address systems and pillow speakers it should be very easy to keep the inmates of even an understaffed institution constantly reminded of this primordial fact. Perhaps a few of the lost souls might in this way be helped to win some measure of control over the Universe—at once beautiful and appalling, but always other than human, always totally incomprehensible-in which they find themselves condemned to live.

None too soon, I was steered away from the disquieting splendours of my garden chair. Drooping in green parabolas from the hedge, the ivy fronds shone with a kind of glassy, jade-like radiance. A moment later a clump of Red Hot Pokers, in full bloom, had exploded into my field of vision. So passionately alive that they seemed to be standing on the very brink of utterance, the flowers strained upwards into the blue. Like the chair under the laths, they protected too much. I looked down at the leaves and discovered a cavernous intricacy of the most delicate green lights and shadows, pulsing with undecipherable mystery.

Roses : The flowers are easy to paint, The leaves difficult.

Shiki's haiku (which I quote in R. H. Blyth's translation) expresses, by indirection, exactly what I then felt—the excessive, the too obvious glory of the flowers, as contrasted with the subtler miracle of their foliage.

We walked out into the street. A large pale blue automobile was standing at the curb. At the sight of it, I was suddenly overcome by enormous merriment. What complacency, what an absurd self-satisfaction beamed from those bulging surfaces of glossiest enamel! Man had created the thing in his own image—or rather in the image of his favourite character in fiction. I laughed till the tears ran down my cheeks.

We re-entered the house. A meal had been prepared. Somebody, who was not yet identical with myself, fell to with ravenous appetite. From a considerable distance and without much interest, I looked on.

When the meal had been eaten, we got into the car and went for a drive. The effects of the mescalin were already on the decline: but the flowers in the gardens still trembled on the brink of being supernatural, the pepper trees and carobs along the side streets still manifestly belonged to some sacred grove. Eden alternated with Dodona. Yggdrasil with the mystic Rose. And then, abruptly, we were at an intersection, waiting to cross Sunset Boulevard. Before us the cars were rolling by in a steady stream—thousands of them, all bright and shiny like an advertiser's dream and each more ludicrous than the last. Once again I was convulsed with laughter.

The Red Sea of traffic parted at last, and we crossed into another oasis of trees and lawns and roses. In a few minutes we had climbed to a vantage point in the hills, and there was the city spread out beneath us.

Rather disappointingly, it looked very like the city I had seen on other occasions. So far as I was concerned, transfiguration was proportional to distance. The nearer, the more divinely other. This vast, dim panorama was hardly different from itself.

We drove on, and so long as we remained in the hills, with view succeeding distant view, significance was at its everyday level, well below transfiguration point. The magic began to work again only when we turned down into a new suburb and were gliding between two rows of houses. Here, in spite of the peculiar hideousness of the architecture, there were renewals of transcendental otherness, hints of the morning's heaven.

Brick chimneys and green composition roofs glowed in the sunshine, like fragments of the New Jerusalem. And all at once I saw what Guardi had seen and (with what incomparable skill) had so often rendered in his paintings—a stucco wall with a shadow slanting across it, blank but unforgettably beautiful, empty but charged with all the meaning and the mystery of existence. The revelation dawned and was gone again within a fraction of a second. The car had moved on; time was uncovering another manifestation of the eternal Suchness. "Within sameness there is difference. But that difference should be different from sameness is in nowise the intention of all the Buddhas. Their intention is both totality and differentiation." This bank of red and white geraniums, for example—it was entirely different from that stucco wall a hundred yards up the road. But the "is-ness" of both was the same, the eternal quality of their transience was the same.

An hour later, with ten more miles and the visit to the World's Biggest Drug Store safely behind us, we were back at home, and I had returned to that reassuring but profoundly unsatisfactory state known as "being in one's right mind."

That humanity at large will ever be able to dispense with Artificial Paradises seems very unlikely. Most men and women lead lives at the worst so painful, at the best so monotonous, poor and limited that the urge to escape, the longing to transcend themselves if only for a few moments, is and has always been one of the principal appetites of the soul.

Art and religion, carnivals and saturnalia, dancing and listening to oratory—all these have served, in H. G. Wells's phrase, as Doors in the Wall.

And for private, for everyday use there have always been chemical intoxicants. All the vegetable sedatives and narcotics, all the euphorics that grow on trees, the hallucinogens that ripen in berries or can be squeezed from roots—all, without exception, have been known and systematically used by human beings from time immemorial. And to these natural modifiers of consciousness modern science has added its quota of synthetics—chloral, for example, and benzedrine, the bromides and the barbiturates.

Most of these modifiers of consciousness cannot now be taken except under doctor's orders, or else illegally and at considerable risk. For unrestricted use the West has permitted only alcohol and tobacco. All the other chemical Doors in the Wall are labelled Dope, and their unauthorized takers are Fiends.

We now spend a good deal more on drink and smoke than we spend on education. This, of course, is not surprising. The urge to escape from selfhood and the environment is in almost everyone almost all the time.

The urge to do something for the young is strong only in parents, and in them only for the few years during which their children go to school.

Equally unsurprising is the current attitude towards drink and smoke. In spite of the growing army of hopeless alcoholics, in spite of the hundreds of thousands of persons annually maimed or killed by drunken drivers, popular comedians still crack jokes about alcohol and its addicts. And in spite of the evidence linking cigarettes with lung cancer, practically everybody regards tobacco smoking as being hardly less normal and natural than eating. From the point of view of the rationalist utilitarian this may seem odd. For the historian, it is exactly what you would expect. A firm conviction of the material reality of Hell never prevented medieval Christians from doing what their ambition, lust or covetousness suggested. Lung cancer, traffic accidents and the millions of miserable and misery-creating alcoholics are facts even more certain than was, in Dante's day, the fact of the Inferno. But all such facts are remote and unsubstantial compared with the near, felt fact of a craving, here and now, for release or sedation, for a drink or a smoke.

Ours is the age, among other things, of the automobile and of rocketing population. Alcohol is incompatible with safety on the roads, and its production, like that of tobacco, condemns to virtual sterility many millions of acres of the most fertile soil. The problems raised by alcohol and tobacco cannot, it goes without saying, be solved by prohibition. The universal and ever-present urge to self-transcendence is not to be abolished by slamming the currently popular Doors in the Wall. The only reasonable policy is to open other, better doors in the hope of inducing men and women to exchange their old bad habits for new and less harmful ones. Some of these other, better doors will be social and technological in nature, others religious or psychological, others dietetic, educational, athletic. But the need for frequent chemical vacations from intolerable selfhood and repulsive surroundings will undoubtedly remain. What is needed is a new drug which will relieve and console our suffering species without doing more harm in the long run than it does good in the short.

Such a drug must be potent in minute doses and synthesizable. If it does not possess these qualities, its production, like that of wine, beer, spirits and tobacco will interfere with the raising of indispensable food and fibres. It must be less toxic than opium or cocaine, less likely to produce undesirable social consequences than alcohol or the barbiturates, less inimical to heart and lungs than the tars and nicotine of cigarettes. And, on the positive side, it should produce changes in consciousness more interesting, more intrinsically valuable than mere sedation or dreaminess, delusions of omnipotence or release from inhibition.

To most people, mescalin is almost completely innocuous. Unlike alcohol, it does not drive the taker into the kind of uninhibited action which results in brawls, crimes of violence and traffic accidents. A man under the influence of mescalin quietly minds his own business. Moreover, the business he minds is an experience of the most enlightening kind, which does not have to be paid for (and this is surely important) by a compensatory hangover. Of the long-range consequences of regular mescalin taking we know very little. The Indians who consume peyote buttons do not seem to be physically or morally degraded by the habit. However, the available evidence is still scarce and sketchy.**

Although obviously superior to cocaine, opium, alcohol and tobacco, mescalin is not yet the ideal drug. Along with the happily transfigured majority of mescalin takers there is a minority that finds in the drug only hell or purgatory. Moreover, for a drug that is to be used, like alcohol, for general consumption, its effects last for an inconveniently long time. But chemistry and physiology are capable nowadays of practically anything. If the psychologists and sociologists will define the ideal, the neurologists and pharmacologists can be relied upon to discover the means whereby that ideal can be realized or at least (for perhaps this kind of ideal can never, in the very nature of things, be fully realized) more nearly approached than in the wine-bibbing past, the whisky-drinking, marijuana-smoking and barbiturate-swallowing present.

The urge to transcend self-conscious selfhood is, as I have said, a principal appetite of the soul. When, for whatever reason, men and women fail to transcend themselves by means of worship, good works and spiritual exercises, they are apt to resort to religion's chemical surrogates—alcohol and "goof pills" in the modern West, alcohol and opium in the East, hashish in the Mohammedan world, alcohol and marijuana in Central America, alcohol and coca in the Andes, alcohol and the barbiturates in the more up-to-date regions of South America.

In Poisons Sacrés, Ivresses Divines Philippe de Felice has written at length and with a wealth of documentation on the immemorial connection between religion and the taking of drugs. Here, in summary or in direct quotation, are his conclusions. The employment for religious purposes of toxic substances is "extraordinarily widespread.... The practices studied in this volume can be observed in every region of the earth, among primitives no less than among those who have reached a high pitch of civilization. We are there-fore dealing not with exceptional facts, which might justifiably be overlooked, but with a general and, in the widest sense of the word, a human phenomenon, the kind of phenomenon which can-not be disregarded by anyone who is trying to discover what religion is, and what are the deep needs which it must satisfy."

Ideally, everyone should be able to find self-transcendence in some form of pure or applied religion. In practice it seems very unlikely that this hoped for consummation will ever be realized. There are, and doubtless there always will be, good churchmen and good churchwomen for whom, unfortunately, piety is not enough. The late G. K. Chesterton, who wrote at least as lyrically of drink as of devotion, may serve as their eloquent spokesman.

The modern churches, with some exceptions among the Protestant denominations, tolerate alcohol; but even the most tolerant have made no attempt to convert the drug to Christianity, or to sacramentalize its use. The pious drinker is forced to take his religion in one compartment, his religion-surrogate in another. And perhaps this is inevitable. Drinking cannot be sacramentalized except in religions which set no store on decorum. The worship of Dionysos or the Celtic god of beer was a loud and disorderly affair. The rites of Christianity are incompatible with even religious drunkenness. This does no harm to the distillers, but is very bad for Christianity. Countless persons desire self-transcendence and would be glad to find it in church. But, alas, "the hungry sheep look up and are not fed." They take part in rites, they listen to sermons, they repeat prayers; but their thirst remains unassuaged. Disappointed, they turn to the bottle.

For a time at least and in a kind of way, it works. Church may still be attended; but it is no more than the Musical Bank of Butler's Erewhon.

God may still be acknowledged; but He is God only on the verbal level, only in a strictly Pickwickian sense. The effective object of worship is the bottle and the sole religious experience is that state of uninhibited and belligerent euphoria which follows the ingestion of the third cocktail.

We see, then, that Christianity and alcohol do not and cannot mix.

Christianity and mescalin seem to be much more compatible. This has been demonstrated by many tribes of Indians, from Texas to as far north as Wisconsin. Among these tribes are to be found

33

groups affiliated with the Native American Church, a sect whose principal rite is a kind of Early Christian agape, or love feast, where slices of peyote take the place of the sacramental bread and wine. These Native Americans regard the cactus as God's special gift to the Indians, and equate its effects with the workings of the divine Spirit.

Professor J. S. Slotkin, one of the very few white men ever to have participated in the rites of a Peyotist congregation, says of his fellow worshipers that they are "certainly not stupefied or drunk.... They never get out of rhythm or fumble their words, as a drunken or stupefied man would do.... They are all quiet, courteous and considerate of one another. I have never been in any white man's house of worship where there is either so much religious feeling or decorum." And what, we may ask, are these devout and well-behaved Peyotists experiencing? Not the mild sense of virtue which sustains the average Sunday churchgoer through ninety minutes of boredom. Not even those high feelings, inspired by thoughts of the Creator and the Redeemer, the Judge and the Comforter, which animate the pious. For these Native Americans, religious experience is something more direct and illuminating, more spontaneous, less the homemade product of the superficial, self-conscious mind. Sometimes (according to the reports collected by Dr. Slotkin) they see visions, which may be of Christ Himself. Sometimes they hear the voice of the Great Spirit. Sometimes they become aware of the presence of God and of those personal short-comings which must be corrected if they are to do His will.

The practical consequences of these chemical openings of doors into the Other World seem to be wholly good. Dr. Slotkin reports that habitual Peyotists are on the whole more industrious, more temperate (many of them abstain altogether from alcohol), more peaceable than non-Peyotists. A tree with such satisfactory fruits cannot be condemned out of hand as evil.

In sacramentalizing the use of peyote, the Indians of the Native American Church have done something which is at once psycho-logically sound and historically respectable. In the early centuries of Christianity many pagan rites and festivals were baptized, so to say, and made to serve the purposes of the Church. These jolli-fications were not particularly edifying; but they assuaged a certain psychological hunger and, instead of trying to suppress them, the earlier missionaries had the sense to accept them for what they were, soul-satisfying expressions of fundamental urges, and to

34

incorporate them into the fabric of the new religion. What the Native Americans have done is essentially similar. They have taken a pagan custom (a custom, incidentally, far more elevating and enlightening than most of the rather brutish carousals and mummeries adopted from European paganism) and given it a Christian significance.

Though but recently introduced into the northern United States, peyote-eating and the religion based upon it have become important symbols of the red man's right to spiritual independence. Some Indians have reacted to white supremacy by becoming Americanized, others by retreating into traditional Indianism. But some have tried to make the best of both worlds, indeed of all the worlds—the best of Indianism, the best of Christianity, and the best of those Other Worlds of transcendental experience, where the soul knows itself as unconditioned and of like nature with the divine. Hence the Native American Church. In it two great appetites of the soul—the urge to independence and self-determination and the urge to self-transcendence—were fused with, and interpreted in the light of, a third—the urge to worship, to justify the ways of God to man, to explain the universe by means of a coherent theology.

Lo, the poor Indian, whose untutored mind Clothes him in front, but leaves him bare behind. But actually it is we, the rich and highly educated whites, who have left ourselves bare behind. We cover our anterior nakedness with some philosophy—Christian, Marxian, Freudo-Physicalist—but abaft we remain uncovered, at the mercy of all the winds of circumstance. The poor Indian, on the other hand, has had the wit to protect his rear by supplementing the fig leaf of a theology with the breechclout of transcendental experience.

I am not so foolish as to equate what happens under the influence of mescalin or of any other drug, prepared or in the future pre-parable, with the realization of the end and ultimate purpose of human life: Enlightenment, the Beatific Vision. All I am suggesting is that the mescalin experience is what Catholic theologians call "a gratuitous grace," not necessary to salvation but potentially helpful and to be accepted thankfully, if made available. To be shaken out of the ruts of ordinary perception, to be shown for a few timeless hours the outer and the inner world, not as they appear to an animal obsessed with survival or to a human being obsessed with words and notions, but as they are apprehended, directly and unconditionally, by Mind at Large—this is an experience of inestimable value to everyone and especially to the intellectual. For the intellectual is by definition the man for whom, in Goethe's phrase, "the word is essentially fruitful." He is the man who feels that "what we perceive by the eye is foreign to us as such and need not impress us deeply." And yet, though himself an intellectual and one of the supreme masters of language, Goethe did not always agree with his own evaluation of the word. "We talk," he wrote in middle life, "far too much. We should talk less and draw more. I personally should like to renounce speech altogether and, like organic Nature, communicate everything I have to say in sketches. That fig tree, this little snake, the cocoon on my window sill quietly awaiting its future—all these are momentous signatures. A person able to decipher their meaning properly would soon be able to dispense with the written or the spoken word altogether. The more I think of it, there is something futile, mediocre, even (I am tempted to say) foppish about speech. By contrast, how the gravity of Nature and her silence startle you, when you stand face to face with her, undistracted, before a barren ridge or in the desolation of the ancient hills." We can never dispense with language and the other symbol systems; for it is by means of them, and only by their means, that we have raised ourselves above the brutes, to the level of human beings. But we can easily become the victims as well as the beneficiaries of these systems. We must learn how to handle words effectively; but at the same time we must preserve and, if necessary, intensify our ability to look at the world directly and not through that half opaque medium of concepts, which distorts every given fact into the all too familiar likeness of some generic label or explanatory abstraction.

Literary or scientific, liberal or specialist, all our education is predominantly verbal and therefore fails to accomplish what it is supposed to do.

Instead of transforming children into fully developed adults, it turns out students of the natural sciences who are completely unaware of Nature as the primary fact of experience, it inflicts upon the world students of the humanities who know nothing of humanity, their own or anyone else's.

Gestalt psychologists, such as Samuel Renshaw, have devised methods for widening the range and increasing the acuity of human perceptions. But do our educators apply them? The answer is, No.

Teachers in every field of psyche-physical skill, from seeing to tennis, from tightrope walking to prayer, have discovered, by trial and error, the conditions of optimum functioning within their special fields. But have any of the great Foundations financed a project for coordinating these empirical findings into a general theory and practice of heightened creativeness? Again, so far as I am aware, the answer is, No.

All sorts of cultists and queer fish teach all kinds of techniques for achieving health, contentment, peace of mind; and for many of their hearers many of these techniques are demonstrably effective. But do we see respectable psychologists, philosophers and clergymen boldly descending into those odd and sometimes malodorous wells, at the bottom of which poor Truth is so often condemned to sit? Yet once more the answer is, No.

And now look at the history of mescalin research. Seventy years ago men of first-rate ability described the transcendental experiences which come to those who, in good health, under proper conditions and in the right spirit, take the drug. How many philosophers, how many theologians, how many professional educators have had the curiosity to open this Door in the Wall? The answer, for all practical purposes, is, None.

In a world where education is predominantly verbal, highly educated people find it all but impossible to pay serious attention to anything but words and notions. There is always money for, there are always doctorates in, the learned foolery of research into what, for scholars, is the all important problem: Who influenced whom to say what when? Even in this age of technology the verbal humanities are honoured. The non-verbal humanities, the arts of being directly aware of the given facts of our existence, are almost completely ignored. A catalogue, a bibliography, a definitive edition of a third-rate versifier's *ipsissima verba*, a stupendous index to end all indexes—any genuinely Alexandrian project is sure of approval and financial support: But when it comes to finding out how you and I, our children and grand-children, may become more perceptive, more intensely aware of inward and outward reality, more open to the Spirit, less apt, by psychological malpractices, to make ourselves physically ill, and more capable of controlling our own autonomic nervous system—when it comes to any form of non-verbal education more fundamental (and more likely to be of some practical use) than Swedish drill, no really respectable person in any really respectable university or church will do anything about it.

Verbalists are suspicious of the non-verbal; rationalists fear the given, non-rational fact; intellectuals feel that "what we perceive by the eye (or in any other way) is foreign to us as such and need not impress us deeply." Besides, this matter of education in the non-verbal humanities will not fit into any of the established pigeon-holes. It is not religion, not neurology, not gymnastics, not morality or civics, not even experimental psychology. This being so the subject is, for academic and ecclesiastical purposes, non-existent and may safely be ignored altogether or left, with a patronizing smile, to those whom the Pharisees of verbal orthodoxy call cranks, quacks, charlatans and unqualified amateurs.

"I have always found," Blake wrote rather bitterly, "that Angels have the vanity to speak of themselves as the only wise. This they do with a confident insolence sprouting from systematic reasoning."

Systematic reasoning is something we could not, as a species or as individuals, possibly do without. But neither, if we are to remain sane, can we possibly do without direct perception, the more unsystematic the better, of the inner and outer worlds into which we have been born.

This given reality is an infinite which passes all understanding and yet admits of being directly and in some sort totally apprehended. It is a transcendence belonging to another order than the human, and yet it maybe present to us as a felt immanence, an experienced participation. To be enlightened is to be aware, always, of total reality in its immanent otherness—to be aware of it and yet to remain in a condition to survive as an animal, to think and feel as a human being, to resort whenever expedient to systematic reasoning. Our goal is to discover that we have always been where we ought to be. Unhappily we make the task exceedingly difficult for ourselves. Meanwhile, however, there are gratuitous graces in the form of partial and fleeting realizations. Under a more realistic, a less exclusively verbal system of education than ours, every Angel (in Blake's sense of that word) would be permitted as a sabbatical treat, would be urged and even, if necessary, compelled to take an occasional trip through some chemical Door in the Wall into the world of transcendental experience. If it terrified him, it would be unfortunate but probably salutary. If it brought him a brief but timeless illumination, so much the better. In either case the Angel might lose a little of the confident insolence sprouting from systematic reasoning and the consciousness of having read all the books.

Near the end of his life Aquinas experienced Infused Contemplation. Thereafter he refused to go back to work on his unfinished book. Compared with this, everything he had read and argued about and written—Aristotle and the Sentences, the Questions, the Propositions, the majestic Summas—was no better than chaff or straw. For most intellectuals such a sit-down strike would be inadvisable, even morally wrong. But the Angelic Doctor had done more systematic reasoning than any twelve ordinary Angels, and was already ripe for death. He had earned the right, in those last months of his mortality, to turn away from merely symbolic straw and chaff to the bread of actual and substantial Fact. For Angels of a lower order and with better prospects of longevity, there must be a return to the straw. But the man who comes back through the Door in the Wall will never be quite the same as the man who went out. He will be wiser but less cocksure, happier but less self-satisfied, humbler in acknowledging his ignorance yet better equipped to understand the relationship of words to things, of systematic reasoning to the unfathomable Mystery which it tries, forever vainly, to comprehend.

Aldous Huxley

NOTES

*See the following papers:
"*Schizophrenia. A New Approach.*" By Humphry Osmond and John Smythies. Journal of Mental Science. Vol. XCVIII. April, 1952.
"*On Being Mad.*" By Humphry Osmond. Saskatchewan Psychiatric Services Journal. Vol. I.
No. 2. September. 1952.
"*The Mescalin Phenomena.*" By John Smythies. The British Journal of the Philosophy of Science. Vol. III. February, 1953.
"*Schizophrenia: A New Approach.*" By Abram Hoffer, Humphry Osmond and John Smythies.
Journal of Mental Science. Vol. C. No. 418. January, 1954.
Numerous other papers on the biochemistry, pharmacology, psychology and neurophysiology of schizophrenia and the mescalin phenomena are in preparation.

**In his monograph, Menomini Peyolism, published (December 1952) in the Transactions of the American Philosophical Society, Professor J. S. Slotkin has written that "the habitual use of Peyote does not seem to produce any increased tolerance or dependence. I know many people who have been Peyotists for forty to fifty years. The amount of Peyote they use depends upon the solemnity of the occasion; in general they do not take any more Peyote now than they did years ago. Also, there is sometimes an interval of a month or more between rites, and they go without Peyote during this period without feeling any craving for it. Personally, even after a series of rites occurring on four successive weekends.
I neither increased the amount of Peyote consumed nor felt any continued need for it." It is evidently with good reason that "Peyote has never been legally declared a narcotic, or its use prohibited by the federal government." However, "during the long history of Indian white contact, white officials have usually tried to suppress the use of Peyote, because it has been conceived to violate their own mores. But these at-tempts have always failed."
In a footnote Dr. Slotkin adds that "it is amazing to hear the fantastic stories about the effects of Peyote and the nature of the ritual, which are told by the white and Catholic Indian officials in the Menomini Reservation. None of them have had the slightest first-hand experience with the plant or with the religion, yet some fancy themselves to be authorities and write official reports on the subject."

HEAVEN
AND
HELL

Foreword

THIS little book is a sequel to an essay on the mescalin experience, published two years ago under the title of The Doors of Perception. For a person in whom 'the candle of vision' never burns spontaneously, the mescalin experience is doubly illuminating. It throws light on the hitherto unknown regions of his own mind; and at the same time it throws light, indirectly, on other minds, more richly gifted in respect to vision than his own.

Reflecting on his experience, he comes to a new and better understanding of the ways in which those other minds perceive and feel and think, of the cosmological notions which seem to them self-evident, and of the works of art through which they feel impelled to express themselves.

In what follows I have tried to set down, more or less systematically, the results of this new understanding.

Aldous Huxley

HEAVEN
AND
HELL

IN the history of science the collector of specimens preceded the zoologist and followed the exponents of natural theology and magic. He had ceased to study animals in the spirit of the authors of the Bestiaries, for whom the ant was incarnate industry, the panther an emblem, surprisingly enough, of Christ, the polecat a shocking example of uninhibited lasciviousness. But, except in a rudimentary way, he was not yet a physiologist, ecologist, or student of animal behaviour. His primary concern was to make a census, to catch, kill, stuff, and describe as many kinds of beasts as he could lay his hands on.

Like the earth of a hundred years ago, our mind still has its darkest Africas, its unmapped Borneos and Amazonian basins. In relation to the fauna of these regions we are not yet zoologists, we are mere naturalists and collectors of specimens. The fact is unfortunate; but we have to accept it, we have to make the best of it. However lowly, the work of the collector must be done, before we can proceed to the higher scientific tasks of classification, analysis, experiment, and theory making.

Like the giraffe and the duck-billed platypus, the creatures inhabiting these remoter regions of the mind are exceedingly improbable. Nevertheless they exist, they are facts of observation; and as such, they cannot be ignored by anyone who is honestly trying to understand the world in which he lives.

It is difficult, it is all but impossible, to speak of mental events except in similes drawn from the more familiar universe of material things. If I have made use of geographical and zoological metaphors, it is not wantonly, out of a mere addiction to picturesque language. It is because such metaphors express very forcibly the essential otherness of the mind's far continents, the complete autonomy and self-sufficiency of their inhabitants. A man consists of what I may call an Old World of personal consciousness and, beyond a dividing sea, a series of New Worlds - the not too distant Virginias and Carolinas of the personal subconscious and the vegetative soul; the Far West of the collective unconscious, with its

42

flora of symbols, its tribes of aboriginal archetypes; and, across another, vaster ocean, at the antipodes of everyday consciousness, the world of Visionary Experience.

If you go to New South Wales, you will see marsupials hopping about the countryside. And if you go to the antipodes of the self-conscious mind, you will encounter all sorts of creatures at least as odd as kangaroos. You do not invent these creatures any more than you invent marsupials. They live their own lives in complete independence. A man cannot control them. All he can do is to go to the mental equivalent of Australia and look around him.

Some people never consciously discover their antipodes. Others make an occasional landing. Yet others (but they are few) find it easy to go and come as they please. For the naturalist of the mind, the collector of psychological specimens, the primary need is some safe, easy, and reliable method of transporting himself and others from the Old World to the New, from the continent of familiar cows and horses to the continent of the wallaby and the platypus.

Two such methods exist. Neither of them is perfect; but both are sufficiently reliable, sufficiently easy, and sufficiently safe to justify their employment by those who know what they are doing. In the first case the soul is transported to its far-off destination by the aid of a chemical - either mescalin or lysergic acid. In the second case, the vehicle is psychological in nature, and the passage to the mind's antipodes is accomplished by hypnosis. The two vehicles carry the consciousness to the same region; but the drug has the longer range and takes its passengers further into the terra incognita. (See Appendix I).

How and why does hypnosis produce its observed effects? We do not know. For our present purposes, however, we do not have to know. All that is necessary, in this context, is to record the fact that some hypnotic subjects are transported, in the trance state, to a region in the mind's antipodes, where they find the equivalent of marsupials - strange psychological creatures leading an autonomous existence according to the law of their own being.

About the physiological effects of mescalin we know a little. Probably (for we are not yet certain) it interferes with the enzyme system that regulates cerebral functioning. By doing so it lowers the efficiency of the brain as an instrument for focusing mind on the problems of life on the surface of our planet. This lowering of what may be called the biological efficiency of the brain seems to permit the entry into consciousness of certain classes of mental events, which are normally excluded, because they possess no survival value. Similar intrusions of biologically useless, but aesthetically and sometimes spiritually valuable, material may occur as the result of illness or fatigue; or they may be induced by fasting, or a period of confinement in a place of darkness and complete silence. (See Appendix II.)

A person under the influence of mescalin or lysergic acid will stop seeing visions when given a large dose of nicotinic acid. This helps to explain the effectiveness of fasting as an inducer of visionary experience. By reducing the amount of available sugar, fasting lowers the brain's biological efficiency and so makes possible the entry into consciousness of material possessing no survival value. Moreover, by causing a vitamin deficiency, it removes from the blood that known inhibitor of visions, nicotinic acid. Another inhibitor of visionary experience is ordinary, everyday, perceptual experience. Experimental psychologists have found that, if you confine a man to a 'restricted environment', where there is no light, no sound, nothing to smell, and, if you put him in a tepid bath with only one almost imperceptible thing to touch, the victim will very soon start 'seeing things', 'hearing things', and having strange bodily sensations.

Milarepa, in his Himalayan cavern, and the anchorites of the Thebaid followed essentially the same procedure and got essentially the same results. A thousand pictures of the Temptations of St Anthony bear witness to the effectiveness of restricted diet and restricted environment. Asceticism, it is evident, has a double motivation. If men and women torment their bodies, it is not only because they hope in this way to atone for past sins and avoid future punishments; it is because they long to visit the mind's antipodes and do some visionary sightseeing. Empirically and from the reports of other ascetics, they know that fasting and a restricted environment will transport them where they long to go. Their self-inflicted punishment may be the door to paradise. (It may also - and this is a point which will be discussed in a later paragraph - be a door into the infernal regions.)

From the point of view of an inhabitant of the Old World, marsupials are exceedingly odd. But oddity is not the same as randomness. Kangaroos and wallabies may lack verisimilitude; but their improbability repeats itself and obeys recognizable laws. The same is true of the psychological creatures inhabiting the remoter regions of our minds. The experiences encountered under the influ-

44

ence of mescalin or deep hypnosis are certainly strange; but they are strange with a certain regularity, strange according to a pattern.

What are the common features which the pattern imposes upon our visionary experiences? First and most important is the experience of light. Everything seen by those who visit the mind's antipodes is brilliantly illuminated and seems to shine from within. All colours are intensified to a pitch far beyond anything seen in the normal state, and at the same time the mind's capacity for recognizing fine distinctions of tone and hue is notably heightened.

In this respect there is a marked difference between these visionary experiences and ordinary dreams. Most dreams are without colour, or else are only partially or feebly coloured. On the other hand, the visions met with under the influence of mescalin or hypnosis are always intensely and, one might say, praeternaturally brilliant in colour. Professor Calvin Hall, who has collected records of many thousands of dreams, tells us that about two-thirds of all dreams are in black and white. 'Only one dream in three is coloured, or has some colour in it.' A few people dream entirely in colour; a few never experience colour in their dreams; the majority sometimes dream in colour, but more often do not.

'We have come to the conclusion,' writes Dr Hall, 'that colour in dreams yields no information about the personality of the dreamer.' I agree with this conclusion. Colour in dreams and visions tells us no more about the personality of the beholder than does colour in the external world. A garden in July is perceived as brightly coloured. The perception tells us something about sunshine, flowers, and butterflies, but little or nothing about our own selves. In the same way the fact that we see brilliant colours in our visions and in some of our dreams tells us something about the fauna of the mind's antipodes, but nothing whatever about the personality who inhabits what I have called the Old World of the mind.

Most dreams are concerned with the dreamer's private wishes and instinctive urges, and with the conflicts which arise when these wishes and urges are thwarted by a disapproving conscience or a fear of public opinion. The story of these drives and conflicts is told in terms of dramatic symbols, and in most dreams the symbols are uncoloured. Why should this be the case? The answer, I presume, is that, to be effective, symbols do not require to be coloured. The letters in which we write about roses need not be red, and we can describe the rainbow by means of ink marks on white paper. Textbooks are illustrated by line engravings and half-tone plates; and these uncoloured images and diagrams effectively convey information.

What is good enough for the waking consciousness is evidently good enough for the personal subconscious, which finds it possible to express its meanings through uncoloured symbols. Colour turns out to be a kind of touchstone of reality. That which is given is coloured; that which our symbol-creating intellect and fancy put together is un-coloured. Thus the external world is perceived as coloured. Dreams, which are not given but fabricated by the personal subconscious, are generally in black and white. (It is worth remarking that, in most people's experience, the most brightly coloured dreams are those of landscapes, in which there is no drama, no symbolic reference to conflict, merely the presentation to consciousness of a given, non-human fact.)

The images of the archetypal world are symbolic; but since we, as individuals, do not fabricate them, but find them 'out there' in the collective unconscious, they exhibit some at least of the characteristics of given reality and are coloured. The non-symbolic inhabitants of the mind's antipodes exist in their own right, and like the given facts of the external world are coloured. Indeed, they are far more intensely coloured than external data. This may be explained, at least in part, by the fact that our perceptions of the external world are habitually clouded by the verbal notions in terms of which we do our thinking. We are forever attempting to convert things into signs for the most intelligible abstractions of our own invention. But in doing so, we rob these things of a great deal of their native thinghood.

At the antipodes of the mind, we are more or less completely free of language, outside the system of conceptual thought. Consequently our perception of visionary objects possesses all the freshness, all the naked intensity, of experiences which have never been verbalized, never assimilated to lifeless abstractions. Their colour (that hallmark of given-ness) shines forth with a brilliance which seems to us praeternatural, because it is in fact entirely natural - entirely natural in the sense of being entirely unsophisticated by language or the scientific, philosophical, and utilitarian notions, by means of which we ordinarily recreate the given world in our own drearily human image.

In his Candle of Vision, the Irish poet A. E. (George Russell) has analysed his visionary experiences with remarkable acuity. 'When I meditate,' he writes, 'I feel in the thoughts and images that throng

46

about me the reflections of personality; but there are also windows in the soul, through which can be seen images created not by human but by the divine imagination.'

Our linguistic habits lead us into error. For example, we are apt to say, 'I imagine', when what we should have said is, 'The curtain was lifted that I might see'. Spontaneous or induced, visions are never our personal property. Memories belonging to the ordinary self have no place in them. The things seen are wholly unfamiliar. 'There is no reference or resemblance', in Sir William Herschel's phrase, 'to any objects recently seen or even thought of.' When faces appear, they are never the faces of friends or acquaintances. We are out of the Old World, and exploring the antipodes.

For most of us most of the time, the world of everyday experience seems rather dim and drab. But for a few people often, and for a fair number occasionally, some of the brightness of visionary experience spills over, as it were, into common seeing, and the everyday universe is transfigured. Though still recognizably itself, the Old World takes on the quality of the mind's antipodes. Here is an entirely characteristic description of this transfiguration of the everyday world.

'I was sitting on the seashore, half listening to a friend arguing violently about something which merely bored me. Unconsciously to myself, I looked at a film of sand I had picked up on my hand, when I suddenly saw the exquisite beauty of every little grain of it; instead of being dull, I saw that each particle was made up on a perfect geometrical pattern, with sharp angles, from each of which a brilliant shaft of light was reflected, while each tiny crystal shone like a rainbow . . . . The rays crossed and recrossed, making exquisite patterns of such beauty that they left me breathless . . . . Then, suddenly, my consciousness was lighted up from within and I saw in a vivid way how the whole universe was made up of particles of material which, no matter how dull and lifeless they might seem, were nevertheless filled with this intense and vital beauty. For a second or two the whole world appeared as a blaze of glory. When it died down, it left me with something I have never forgotten and which constantly reminds me of the beauty locked up in every minute speck of material around us.'

Similarly George Russell writes of seeing the world illumined by 'an intolerable lustre of light'; of finding himself looking at 'landscapes as lovely as a lost Eden'; of beholding a world where the 'colours were brighter and purer, and yet made a softer harmony'.

47

Again, 'the winds were sparkling and diamond clear, and yet full of colour as an opal, as they glittered through the valley, and I knew the Golden Age was all about me, and it was we who had been blind to it, but that it had never passed away from the world.'

Many similar descriptions are to be found in the poets and in the literature of religious mysticism. One thinks, for example, of Wordsworth's *Ode on the Intimations of Immortality in Early Childhood*; of certain lyrics by George Herbert and Henry Vaughan; of Traherne's *Centuries of Meditations*; of the passage in his autobiography, where Father Surin describes the miraculous transformation of an enclosed convent garden into a fragment of heaven. Praeternatural light and colour are common to all visionary experiences. And along -with light and colour there goes, in every case, a recognition of heightened significance. The self-luminous objects which we see in the mind's antipodes possess a meaning, and this meaning is as intense as their colour. Significance here is identical with being; for, at the mind's antipodes, objects do not stand for anything but themselves. The images which appear in the nearer reaches of the collective subconscious have meaning in relation to the basic facts of human experience; but here, at the limits of the visionary world, we are confronted by facts which, like the facts of external nature, are independent of man, both individually and collectively, and exist in their own right. And their meaning consists precisely in this, that they are intensely themselves and, being intensely themselves, are manifestations of the essential given-ness, the non-human otherness of the universe.

Light, colour, and significance do not exist in isolation. They modify, or are manifested by, objects. Are there any special classes of objects common to most visionary experiences ? The answer is: Yes, there are. Under mescalin and hypnosis, as well as in spontaneous visions, certain classes of perceptual experiences turn up again and again.

The typical mescalin or lysergic acid experience begins with perceptions of coloured, moving, living geometrical forms, m time, pure geometry becomes concrete, and the visionary perceives, not patterns, but patterned things, such as carpets, carvings, mosaics. These give place to vast and complicated buildings, in the midst of landscapes, which change continuously, passing from richness to more intensely coloured richness, from grandeur to deepening grandeur. Heroic figures, of the kind that Blake called 'The Seraphim', may make their appearance, alone or in multitudes. Fab-

48

ulous animals move across the scene. Everything is novel and amazing. Almost never does the visionary see anything that reminds him of his own past. He is not remembering scenes, persons, or objects, and he is not inventing them; he is looking on at a new creation.

The raw material for this creation is provided by the visual experiences of ordinary life; but the moulding of this material into forms is the work of someone who is most certainly not the self, who originally had the experiences, or who later recalled and reflected upon them. They are (to quote the words used by Dr J. R. Smythies in a recent paper in the American Journal of Psychiatry) 'the work of a highly differentiated mental compartment, without any apparent connexion, emotional or volitional, with the aims, interests, or feelings of the person concerned'.

Here, in quotation or condensed paraphrase, is Weir Mitchell's account of the visionary world to which he was transported by peyote, the cactus which is the natural source of mescalin.

At his entry into that world he saw a host of 'star points' and what looked like 'fragments of stained glass'. Then came 'delicate floating films of colour'. These were displaced by an 'abrupt rush of countless points of white light', sweeping across the field of vision. Next there were zigzag lines of very bright colours, which somehow turned into swelling clouds of still more brilliant hues. Buildings now made their appearance, and then landscapes. There was a Gothic tower of elaborate design with worn statues in the doorways or on stone brackets. 'As I gazed, every projecting angle, cornice and even the faces of the stones at their joinings were by degrees covered or hung with clusters of what seemed to be huge precious stones, but uncut stones, some being more like masses of transparent fruit. . . . All seemed to possess an interior light.' The Gothic tower gave place to a mountain, a cliff of inconceivable height, a colossal birdclaw carved in stone and projecting over the abyss, an endless unfurling of coloured draperies, and an efflorescence of more precious stones. Finally there was a view of green and purple waves breaking on a beach 'with myriads of lights of the same tint as the waves'.

Every mescalin experience, every vision arising under hypnosis, is unique; but all recognizably belong to the same species. The landscapes, the architectures, the clustering gems, the brilliant and intricate patterns - these, in their atmosphere of praeternatural light, praeternatural colour, and praeternatural significance, are the stuff of which the mind's antipodes are made. Why this should be so, we have no idea. It is a brute fact of experience which, whether we like it or not, we have to accept - just as we have to accept the fact of kangaroos.

From these facts of visionary experience let us now pass to the accounts preserved in all the cultural traditions, of Other Worlds - the worlds inhabited by the gods, by the spirits of the dead, by man in his primal state of innocence.

Reading these accounts, we are immediately struck by the close similarity between induced or spontaneous visionary experience and the heavens and fairylands of folklore and religion. Praeternatural light, praeternatural intensity of colouring, praeternatural significance - these are characteristic of all the Other Worlds and Golden Ages. And in virtually every case this praeternaturally significant light shines on, or shines out of, a landscape of such surpassing beauty that words cannot express it.

Thus in the Greco-Roman tradition we find the lovely Garden of the Hesperides, the Elysian Plain, and the fair Island of Leuke, to which Achilles was translated. Memnon went to another luminous island, somewhere in the East. Odysseus and Penelope travelled in the opposite direction and enjoyed their immortality with Circe in Italy. Still further to the West were the Islands of the Blest, first mentioned by Hesiod and so firmly believed in that, as late as the first century B.C., Sertorius planned to send a squadron from Spain to discover them.

Magically lovely islands reappear in the folklore of the Celts and, at the opposite side of the world, in that of the Japanese. And between Avalon in the extreme West and Horaisan in the Far East, there is the land of Uttarakuru, the Other World of the Hindus. 'The land,' we read in the Ramayana, 'is watered by lakes with golden lotuses. There are rivers by thousands, full of leaves of the colour of sapphire and lapis lazuli; and the lakes, resplendent like the morning sun, are adorned by golden beds of red lotus. The country all around is covered by jewels and precious stones, with gay beds of blue lotus, golden-petalled. Instead of sand, pearls, gems, and gold form the banks of the rivers, which are overhung with trees of fire-bright gold. These trees perpetually bear flowers and fruit, give forth a sweet fragrance and abound with birds."

Uttarakuru, we see, resembles the landscapes of the mescalin experience in being rich with precious stones. And this characteristic is common to virtually all the Other Worlds of religious tradition. Every paradise abounds in gems, or at least in gem-like objects resembling, as Weir Mitchell puts it, 'transparent fruit'. Here, for example, is Ezekiel's version of the Garden of Eden. 'Thou hast been in Eden, the garden of God. Every precious stone was thy covering, the sardius, topaz and the diamond, the beryl, the onyx and the jasper, the sapphire, the emerald and the carbuncle, and gold. . . . Thou art the anointed cherub that covereth . . . thou hast walked up and down in the midst of the stones of fire.' The Buddhist paradises are adorned with similar 'stones of fire". Thus, the Western Paradise of the Pure Land Sect is walled with silver, gold, and beryl; has lakes with jewelled banks and a profusion of glowing lotuses, within which the Bodhisattvas sit enthroned.

In describing their Other Worlds, the Celts and Teutons speak very little of precious stones, but have much to say of another and, for them, equally wonderful substance - glass. The Welsh had a blessed land called Ynisvitrin, the Isle of Glass; and one of the names of the Germanic kingdom of the dead was Glasberg. One is reminded of the Sea of Glass in the Apocalypse.

Most paradises are adorned with buildings, and, like the trees, the waters, the hills and fields, these buildings are bright with gems. We are all familiar with the New Jerusalem. 'And the building of the wall of it was of jasper, and the city was of pure gold, like unto clear glass. And the foundations of the wall of the city were garnished with all manner of precious stones.'

Similar descriptions are to be found in the eschatological literature of Hinduism, Buddhism, and Islam. Heaven is always a place of gems. Why should this be the case? Those who think of all human activities in terms of a social and economic frame of reference will give some such answer as this: Gems are very rare on earth. Few people possess them. To compensate themselves for these facts, the spokesmen for the poverty-stricken majority have filled their imaginary heavens with precious stones. This 'pie in the sky' hypothesis contains, no doubt, some element of truth; but it fails to explain why precious stones should have come to be regarded as precious in the first place.

Men have spent enormous amounts of time, energy, and money on the finding, mining, and cutting of coloured pebbles. Why? The utilitarian can offer no explanation for such fantastic behaviour. But as soon as we take into account the facts of visionary experience, everything becomes clear. In vision, men perceive a profusion of what Ezekiel calls 'stones of fire', of what Weir Mitchell describes as 'transparent fruit'. These things are self-luminous, exhibit a praeternatural brilliance of colour and possess a praeternatural significance. The material objects which most nearly resemble these sources of visionary illumination are gem-stones. To acquire such a stone is to acquire something whose preciousness is guaranteed by the fact that it exists in the Other World.

Hence man's otherwise inexplicable passion for gems and hence his attribution to precious stones of therapeutic and magical virtue. The causal chain, I am convinced, begins in the psychological Other World of visionary experience, descends to earth, and mounts again to the theological Other World of heaven. In this context the words of Socrates, in the Phaedo, take on a new significance. There exists, he tells us, an ideal world above and beyond the world of matter. In this other earth the colours are much purer and much more brilliant than they are down here. ... The very mountains, the very stones have a richer gloss, a lovelier transparency and intensity of hue. The precious stones of this lower world, our highly prized cornelians, jaspers, emeralds, and all the rest, are but the tiny fragments of these stones above. In the other earth there is no stone but is precious and exceeds in beauty every gem of ours."

In other words, precious stones are precious because they bear a faint resemblance to the glowing marvels seen with the inner eye of the visionary. 'The view of that world,' says Plato, 'is a vision of blessed beholders'; for to see things 'as they are in themselves' is bliss unalloyed and inexpressible.

Among people who have no knowledge of precious stones or of glass, heaven is adorned not with minerals, but flowers. Praeternaturally brilliant flowers bloom in most of the Other Worlds described by primitive eschatologists, and even in the begemmed and glassy paradises of the more advanced religions they have their place. One remembers the lotus of Hindu and Buddhist tradition, the roses and lilies of the West.

'God first planted a garden.' The statement expresses a deep psychological truth. Horticulture has its source - or at any rate one of its sources - in the Other World of the mind's antipodes. When worshippers offer flowers at the altar, they are returning to the gods things which they know, or (if they are not visionaries) obscurely feel, to be indigenous to heaven.

And this return to the source is not merely symbolical; it is also a matter of immediate experience. For the traffic between our Old World and its antipodes, between Here and Beyond, travels along a two-way street. Gems, for example, come from the soul's visionary heaven; but they also lead the soul back to that heaven. Contemplating them, men find themselves (as the phrase goes) transported-carried away towards that Other Earth of the Platonic dialogue, the magical place where every pebble is a precious stone. And the same effects may be produced by artefacts of glass and metal, by tapers burning in the dark, by brilliantly coloured images and ornaments, by flowers, shells, and feathers, by landscapes seen, as Shelley from the Euganean Hills saw Venice, in the transfiguring light of dawn or sunset.

Indeed, we may risk a generalization and say that whatever, in nature or in a work of art, resembles one of those intensely significant, inwardly glowing objects encountered at the mind's antipodes, is capable of inducing, if only in a partial and attenuated form, the visionary experience. At this point a hypnotist will remind us that, if he can be induced to stare intently at a shiny object, a patient may go into trance; and that if he goes into trance, or if he goes only into reverie, he may very well see visions within and a transfigured world without.

But how, precisely, and why does the view of a shiny object induce a trance or a state of reverie? Is it, as the Victorians maintained, a simple matter of eye strain resulting in general nervous exhaustion? Or shall we explain the phenomenon in purely psychological terms - as concentration pushed to the point of monoideism and leading to dissociation?

But there is a third possibility. Shiny objects may remind our unconscious of what it enjoys at the mind's antipodes, and these obscure intimations of life in the Other World are so fascinating that we pay less attention to this world and so become capable of experiencing consciously something of that which, unconsciously, is always with us.

We see then that there are in nature certain scenes, certain classes of objects, certain materials, possessed of the power to transport the beholder's mind in the direction of its antipodes, out of the everyday Here and towards the Other World of Vision. Similarly, in the realm of art, we find certain works, even certain classes of works, in which the same transporting power is manifest. These vision-inducing works may be executed in vision-inducing materials, such as glass, metal, gems, or gem-like pigments. In other cases their power is due to the fact that they render, in some peculiarly expressive way, some transporting scene or object.

The best vision-inducing art is produced by men and women who have themselves had the visionary experience; but it is also possible for any reasonably good artist, simply by following an approved recipe, to create works which shall have at least some transporting power.

Of all the vision-inducing arts that which depends most completely on its raw materials is, of course, the art of the goldsmith and jeweller. Polished metals and precious stones are so intrinsically transporting that even a Victorian, even an Art Nouveau jewel is a thing of power. And when to this natural magic of glinting metal and self-luminous stone is added the other magic of noble forms and colours artfully blended, we find ourselves in the presence of a genuine talisman.

Religious art has always and everywhere made use of these vision-inducing materials. The shrine of gold, the chryselephantine statue, the jewelled symbol or image, the glittering furniture of the altar - we find these things in contemporary Europe as in ancient Egypt, in India and China as among the Greeks, the Incas, the Aztecs.

The products of the goldsmith's art are intrinsically numinous. They have their place at the very heart of every Mystery, in every holy of holies. This sacred jewellery has always been associated with the light of lamps and candles. For Ezekiel, a gem was a stone of fire. Conversely, a flame is a living gem, endowed with all the transporting power that belongs to the precious stone and, to a lesser degree, to polished metal. This transporting power of flame increases in proportion to the depth and extent of the surrounding darkness. The most impressively numinous temples are caverns of twilight, in which a few tapers give life to the transporting, otherworldly treasures on the altar.

Glass is hardly less effective as an inducer of visions than are the natural gems. In certain respects it is more effective, for the simple reason that there is more of it. Thanks to glass, a whole building - the Sainte-Chapelle, for example, the cathedrals of Chartres and Sens - could be turned into something magical and transporting. Thanks to glass, Paolo Uccello could design a circular jewel thirteen feet in diameter - his great window of the Resurrection, perhaps the most extraordinary single work of vision-inducing art ever produced.

For the men of the Middle Ages, it is evident, visionary experience was supremely valuable. So valuable, indeed, that they were

ready to pay for it in hard-earned cash. In the twelfth century col-
lecting-boxes were placed in the churches for the upkeep and
installation of stained-glass windows. Suger, the Abbot of Saint-
Denis, tells us that they were always full but self-respecting artists
cannot be expected to go on doing what their fathers have already
done supremely well. In the fourteenth century colour gave place
to grisaille, and windows ceased to be vision-inducing. When, in
the later fifteenth century, colour came into fashion again, the glass
painters felt the desire, and found themselves, at the same time,
technically equipped, to imitate Renaissance painting in transparency. The results were often interesting; but they were not transporting.

Then came the Reformation. The Protestants disapproved of
visionary experience and attributed a magical virtue to the printed
word. In a church with clear windows the worshippers could read
their Bibles and prayer books and were not tempted to escape from
the sermon into the Other World. On the Catholic side the men of
the Counter-Reformation found themselves in two minds. They
thought visionary experience was a good thing, but they also believed in the supreme value of print.

In the new churches stained glass was rarely installed, and in
many of the older churches it was wholly or partially replaced by
clear glass. The unobscured light permitted the faithful to follow
the service in their books, and at the same time to see the vision-
inducing works created by the new generations' of baroque sculp-
tors and architects. These transporting works were executed in
metal and polished stone. Wherever the worshipper turned, he
found the glint of bronze, the rich radiance of coloured marble, the
unearthly whiteness of statuary.

On the rare occasions when the Counter-Reformers made use of
glass, it was as a surrogate for diamonds, not for rubies or sap-
phires. Faceted prisms entered religious art in the seventeenth
century, and in Catholic churches they dangle to this day from
innumerable chandeliers. (These charming and slightly ridiculous
ornaments are among the very few vision-inducing devices permitted in Islam. Mosques have no images or reliquaries; but in the
Near East, at any rate, their austerity is sometimes mitigated by the
transporting glitter of rococo crystal.)

From glass, stained or cut, we pass to marble and the other
stones that take a high polish and can be used in mass. The fascination exercised by such stones may be gauged by the amount of

time and trouble spent in obtaining them. At Baalbek, for example, and, two or three hundred miles further inland, at Palmyra, we find among the ruins columns of pink granite from Aswan. These great monoliths were quarried in Upper Egypt, were floated in barges down the Nile, were towed across the Mediterranean to Byblos or Tripolis, and from thence were hauled, by oxen, mules, and men, uphill to Horns, and from Horns southward to Baalbek or east, across the desert, to Palmyra.

What a labour of giants! And, from the utilitarian point of view, how marvellously pointless! But, of course, there was a point - a point that existed in a region beyond mere utility. Polished to a visionary glow, the rosy shafts proclaimed their manifest kinship with the Other World. At the cost of enormous efforts men had transported these stones from their quarry on the Tropic of Cancer; and now, by way of recompense, the stones were transporting their transporters half-way to the mind's visionary antipodes.

The question of utility and of the motives that lie beyond utility arises once more in relation to ceramics. Few things are more useful, more absolutely indispensable, than pots and plates and jugs. But at the same time few human beings concern themselves less with utility than do the collectors of porcelain and glazed earthenware. To say that these people have an appetite for beauty is not a sufficient explanation. The commonplace ugliness of the surroundings in which fine ceramics are so often displayed is proof enough that what their owners crave is not beauty in all its manifestations, but only a special kind of beauty - the beauty of curved reflections, of softly lustrous glazes, of sleek and smooth surfaces. In a word, the beauty that transports the beholder, because it reminds him, obscurely or explicitly, of the praeternatural lights and colours of the Other World. In the main the art of the potter has been a secular art - but a secular art which its innumerable devotees have treated with an almost idolatrous reverence. From time to time, however, this secular art has been placed at the service of religion. Glazed tiles have found their way into mosques and, here and there, into Christian churches. From China come shining ceramic images of gods and saints. In Italy Luca della Robbia created a heaven of blue glaze, for his lustrous white madonnas and Christ children. Baked clay is cheaper than marble and, suitably treated, almost as transporting.

Plato and, during a later flowering of religious art, St Thomas Aquinas maintained that pure, bright colours were of the very essence of artistic beauty. A Matisse, in that case, would be intrinsically superior to a Goya or a Rembrandt. One has only to translate the philosophers' abstractions into concrete terms to see that this equation of beauty in general with bright, pure colours is absurd. But though untenable as it stands, the venerable doctrine is not altogether devoid of truth.

Bright, pure colours are characteristic of the Other World. Consequently works of art painted in bright, pure colours are capable, in suitable circumstances, of transporting the beholder's mind in the direction of its antipodes. Bright pure colours are of the essence, not of beauty in general, but only of a special kind of beauty, the visionary. Gothic churches and Greek temples, the statues of the thirteenth century after Christ and of the fifth century before Christ - all were brilliantly coloured.

For the Greeks and the men of the Middle Ages, this art of the merry-go-round and the wax-work show was evidently transporting. To us it seems deplorable. We prefer our Praxiteleses plain, our marble and our limestone *au naturel*. Why should our modern taste be so different, in this respect, from that of our ancestors? The reason, I presume, is that we have become too familiar with bright pure pigments to be greatly moved by them. We admire them, of course, when we see them in some grand or subtle composition; but in themselves and as such, they leave us untransported.

Sentimental lovers of the past complain of the drabness of our age and contrast it unfavourably with the gay brilliance of earlier times. In actual fact, of course, there is a far greater profusion of colour in the modern than in the ancient world. Lapis lazuli and Tynan purple were costly rarities; the rich velvets and brocades of princely wardrobes, the woven or painted hangings of medieval and early modern houses, were reserved for a privileged minority.

Even the great ones of the earth possessed very few of these vision-inducing treasures. As late as the seventeenth century, monarchs owned so little furniture that they had to travel from palace to palace with wagon-loads of plate and bedspreads, of carpets and tapestries. For the great mass of the people there were only homespun and a few vegetable dyes; and, for interior decoration, there were at best the earth colours, at worst (and in most cases) 'the floor of plaster and the walls of dung".

At the antipodes of every mind lay the Other World of praeternatural light and praeternatural colour, of ideal gems and visionary gold. But before every pair of eyes was only the dark squalor of the family hovel, the dust or mud of the village street, the dirty whites, the duns and goose-turd greens of ragged clothing. Hence a passionate, an almost desperate, thirst for bright, pure colours; and hence the overpowering effect produced by such colours whenever, in church or at court, they were displayed. Today the chemical industry turns out paints, inks, and dyes in endless variety and enormous quantities. In our modern world there is enough bright colour to guarantee the production of billions of flags and comic strips, millions of stop signs and tail-lights, fire engines and Coca-Cola containers by the hundred thousand, carpets, wallpapers, and non-representational art by the square mile.

Familiarity breeds indifference. We have seen too much pure, bright colour at Woolworth's to find it intrinsically transporting. And here we may note that, by its amazing capacity to give us too much of the best things, modern technology has tended to devaluate the traditional vision-inducing materials. The illumination of a city, for example, was once a rare event, reserved for victories and national holidays, for the canonization of saints and the crowning of kings. Now it occurs nightly and celebrates the virtues of gin, cigarettes, and toothpaste.

In London, fifty years ago, electric sky signs were a novelty, and so rare that they shone out of the misty darkness 'like captain jewels in the carcanet'. Across the Thames, on the old Shot Tower, the gold and ruby letters were magically lovely - *une feerie*. To-day the fairies are gone. Neon is everywhere and, being everywhere, has no effect upon us, except perhaps to make us pine nostalgically for primeval night.

Only in floodlighting do we recapture the unearthly significance which used, in the age of oil and wax, even in the age of gas and the carbon filament, to shine forth from practically any island of brightness in the boundless dark. Under the searchlights Notre-Dame de Paris and the Roman Forum are visionary objects, having power to transport the beholder's mind towards the Other World. (See Appendix III.)

Modern technology has had the same devaluating effect on glass and polished metal as it has had on fairy lamps and pure, bright colours. By John of Patmos and his contemporaries, walls of glass were conceivable only in the New Jerusalem. To-day they are a feature of every up-to-date office building and bungalow. And this glut of glass has been paralleled by a glut of chrome and nickel, of stainless steel and aluminium and a host of alloys old and new. Metal surfaces wink at us in the bathroom, shine from the kitchen sink, go glittering across country in cars and trams.

Those rich convex reflections, which so fascinated Rembrandt that he never tired of rendering them in paint, are now the commonplaces of home and street and factory. The fine point of seldom pleasure has been blunted. What was once a needle of visionary delight has now become a piece of disregarded linoleum.

I have spoken so far only of vision-inducing materials and their psychological devaluation by modern technology. It is time now to consider the purely artistic devices, by means of which vision-inducing works have been created.

Light and colour tend to take on a praeternatural quality when seen in the midst of environing darkness. Fra Angelico's Crucifixion at the Louvre has a black background. So have the frescoes of the Passion painted by Andrea del Castagno for the nuns of Santa Apollonia at Florence. Hence the visionary intensity, the strange transporting power of these extraordinary works. In an entirely different artistic and psychological context the same device was often used by Goya in his etchings. Those flying men, that horse on a tightrope, the huge and ghastly incarnation of Fear - all of them stand out, as though floodlit, against a background of impenetrable night.

With the development of chiaroscuro, in the sixteenth and seventeenth centuries, night came out of the background and installed itself within the picture, which became the scene of a kind of Manichean struggle between Light and Darkness. At the time they were painted these works must have possessed a real transporting power. To us, who have seen altogether too much of this kind of thing, most of them seem merely theatrical. But a few still retain their magic. There is Caravaggio's Entombment, for example; there are a dozen magical paintings by Georges de La Tour (See Appendix IV); there are all those visionary Rembrandts where the lights have the intensity and significance of light at the mind's antipodes, where the darks are full of rich potentialities waiting their turn to become actual, to make themselves glowingly present to our consciousness.

In most cases the ostensible subject-matter of Rembrandt's pictures is taken from real life or the Bible - a boy at his lessons or Bathsheba bathing; a woman wading in a pond or Christ before His judges. Occasionally, however, these messages from the Other

World are transmitted by means of a subject drawn, not from real life or history, but from the realm of archetypal symbols. There hangs in the Louvre a *Meditation du philosophe*, whose symbolical subject-matter is nothing more nor less than the human mind, with its teeming darknesses, its moments of intellectual and visionary illumination, its mysterious stairways winding downwards and upwards into the unknown. The meditating philosopher sits there in his island of inner illumination; and at the opposite end of the symbolic chamber, in another, rosier island, an old woman crouches before the hearth. The firelight touches and transfigures her face, and we see, concretely illustrated, the impossible paradox and supreme truth - that perception is (or at least can be, ought to be) the same as Revelation, that Reality shines out of every appearance, that the One is totally, infinitely present in all particulars.

Along with the praeternatural lights and colours, the gems and the ever-changing patterns, visitors to the mind's antipodes discover a world of sublimely beautiful landscapes, of living architecture, and of heroic figures. The transporting power of many works of art is attributable to the fact that their creators have painted scenes, persons, and objects which remind the beholder of what, consciously or unconsciously, he knows about the Other World at the back of his mind.

Let us begin with the human or, rather, the more than human inhabitants of these far-off regions. Blake called them the Cherubim. And in effect that is what, no doubt, they are - the psychological originals of those beings who, in the theology of every religion, serve as intermediaries between man and the Clear Light. The more than human personages of visionary experience never 'do anything". (Similarly the blessed never 'do anything' in heaven.) They are content merely to exist.

Under many names and attired in an endless variety of costumes, these heroic figures of man's visionary experience have appeared in the religious art of every culture. Sometimes they are shown at rest, sometimes in historical or mythological action. But action, as we have seen, does not come naturally to the inhabitants of the mind's antipodes. To be busy is the law of our being. The law of theirs is to do nothing. When we force these serene strangers to play a part in one of our all too human dramas, we are being false to visionary truth. That is why the most transporting (though not necessarily the most beautiful) representation of 'the Cherubim' are those which show them as they are in their native habitat - doing nothing in particular.

And that accounts for the overwhelming, the more than merely aesthetic, impression made upon the beholder by the great master-pieces of religious art. The sculptured figures of Egyptian gods and god-kings, the Madonnas and Pantocrators of the Byzantine mos-aics, the Bodhisattvas and Lohans of China, the seated Buddhas of Khmer, the steles and statues of Copan, the wooden idols of tro-pical Africa - these have one characteristic in common: a profound stillness. And it is precisely this which gives them their numinous quality, their power to transport the beholder out of the Old World of his everyday experience, far away, towards the visionary anti-podes of the human psyche.

There is, of course, nothing intrinsically excellent about static art. Static or dynamic, a bad piece of work is always a bad piece of work. All I mean to imply is that, other things being equal, a heroic figure at rest has a greater transporting power than one which is shown in action.

The Cherubim live in Paradise and the New Jerusalem - in other words, among prodigious buildings set in rich, bright gardens with distant prospects of plain and mountain, of rivers and the sea. This is a matter of immediate experience, a psychological fact which has been recorded in folklore and the religious literature of every age and country. It has not, however, been recorded in pictorial art.

Reviewing the succession of human cultures, we find that land-scape painting is either non-existent, or rudimentary, or of very re-cent development. In Europe a full-blown art of landscape painting has existed for only four or five centuries, in China for not more than a thousand years, in India, for all practical purposes, never.

This is a curious fact that demands an explanation. Why should landscapes have found their way into the visionary literature of a given epoch and a given culture, but not into the painting? Posed in this way, the question provides its own best answer. People may be content with the merely verbal expression of this aspect of their visionary experience and feel no need for its translation into pic-torial terms.

That this often happens in die case of individuals is certain. Blake, for example, saw visionary landscapes, 'articulated beyond all that the mortal and perishing nature can produce and 'infinitely more perfect and minutely organized than anything seen by the mortal eye'. Here is the description of such a visionary landscape, which Blake gave at one of Mrs Aders' evening parties: 'The other evening, taking a walk, I came to a meadow and at the further corner of it I saw a fold of lambs. Coming nearer, the ground blushed with flowers, and the wattled cote and its woolly tenants were of an exquisite pastoral beauty. But I looked again, and it proved to be no living flock, but beautiful sculpture.'

Rendered in pigments, this vision would look, I suppose, like some impossibly beautiful blending of one of Constable's freshest oil sketches with an animal painting in the magically realistic style of Zurbaran's haloed lamb now in the San Diego Museum. But Blake never produced anything remotely resembling such a picture. He was content to talk and write about his landscape visions, and to concentrate in his painting upon 'the Cherubim'.

What is true of an individual artist may be true of a whole school. There are plenty of things which men experience, but do not choose to express; or they may try to express what they have experienced, but in only one of their arts. In yet other cases they will express themselves hi ways having no immediately recognizable affinity to the original experience. In this last context Dr A. K. Coomaraswamy has some interesting things to say about the mystical art of the Far East - the art where 'denotation and connotation cannot be divided' and 'no distinction is felt between what a thing "is" and what it "signifies" '.

The supreme example of such mystical art is the Zen-inspired landscape painting, which arose in China during the Sung period and came to new birth in Japan four centuries later. India and the Near East have no mystical landscape painting; but they have its equivalents -' Vaisnava painting, poetry, and music in India, where the theme is sexual love; and Sufi poetry and music in Persia, devoted to praises of intoxication.' (A. K. Coomaraswamy, The Transformation of Nature in Art, p. 40.)

'Bed,' as the Italian proverb succinctly puts it, 'is the poor man's opera.' Analogously, sex is the Hindu's Sung; wine, the Persian's Impressionism. The reason being, of course, that the experiences of sexual union and intoxication partake of that essential otherness characteristic of all vision, including that of landscapes.

If, at any time, men have found satisfaction in a certain kind of activity, it is to be presumed that, at periods when this satisfying activity was not manifested, there must have been some kind of equivalent for it. In the Middle Ages, for example, men were preoccupied in an obsessive, an almost maniacal way with words and symbols. Everything in nature was instantly recognized as the concrete illustration of some notion formulated in one of the books or legends currently regarded as sacred.

And yet, at other periods of history men have found a deep satisfaction in recognizing the autonomous otherness of nature, including many aspects of human nature. The experience of this otherness was expressed in terms of art, religion, or science. What were the medieval equivalents of Constable and ecology, of bird watching and Eleusis, of microscopy and the rites of Dionysos and the Japanese Haiku? They were to be found, I suspect, in Saturnalian orgies at one end of the scale and in mystical experience at the other. Shrovetides, May Days, Carnivals - these permitted a direct experience of the animal otherness underlying personal and social identity. Infused contemplation revealed the yet *otherer* otherness of the divine Not-Self. And somewhere between the two extremes were the experiences of the visionaries and the vision-inducing arts, by means of which it was sought to recapture and re-create those experiences - the art of the jeweller, of the maker of stained glass, of the weaver of tapestries, of the painter, poet, and musician.

In spite of a Natural History that was nothing but a set of drearily moralistic symbols, in the teeth of a theology which, instead of regarding words as the signs of things, treated things and events as the signs of biblical or Aristotelian words, our ancestors remained relatively sane. And they achieved this feat by periodically escaping from the stifling prison of their bumptiously rationalistic philosophy, their anthropomorphic, authoritarian, and non-experimental science, their all too articulate religion, into nonverbal, other than human worlds inhabited by their instincts, by the visionary fauna of their mind's antipodes, and, beyond and yet within all the rest, by the indwelling Spirit.

From this wide-ranging but necessary digression, let us return to the particular case from which we set out. Landscapes, as we have seen, are a regular feature of the visionary experience. Descriptions of visionary landscapes occur in the ancient literature of folklore and religion; but paintings of landscapes do not make their appearance until comparatively recent times. To what has been said, by way of explanation about psychological equivalents, I will add a few brief notes on the nature of landscape paintings as a vision-inducing art. Let us begin by asking a question. "What landscapes - or, more generally, what representations of natural objects - are most transporting, most intrinsically vision-inducing? In the light of my own experiences and of what I have heard other people say about their reactions to works of art, I will risk an answer. Other things being equal (for nothing can make up for lack of talent), the most transporting landscapes are, first, those which represent natural objects a very long way off, and, second, those which represent them at close range.

Distance lends enchantment to the view; but so does propinquity. A Sung painting of far away mountains, clouds, and torrents is transporting; but so are the close-ups of tropical leaves in the Douanier Rousseau's jungles. When I look at the Sung landscape, I am reminded (or one of my not-I's is reminded) of the crags, the boundless expanses of plain, the luminous skies and seas of the mind's antipodes. And those disappearances into mist and cloud, those sudden emergences of some strange, intensely definite form, a weathered rock, for example, an ancient pinetree twisted by years of struggle with the wind - these too, are transporting. For they remind me, consciously or unconsciously, of the Other World's essential alienness and unaccountability.

It is the same with the close-up. I look at those leaves with their architecture of veins, their stripes and mottlings, I peer into the depths of interlacing greenery, and something in me is reminded of those living patterns, so characteristic of the visionary world, of those endless births and proliferations of geometrical forms that turn into objects, of things that are for ever being transmuted into other things.

This painted close-up of a jungle is what, on one of its aspects, the Other World is like, and so it transports me, it makes me see with eyes that transfigure a work of art into something else, something beyond art.

I remember very vividly, though it took place many years ago, a conversation with Roger Fry. We were talking about Monet's Water Lilies. They had no right, Roger kept insisting, to be so shockingly unorganized, so totally without a proper compositional skeleton. They were all wrong, artistically speaking. And yet, he had to admit, and yet . . . . And yet, as I should now say, they were transporting. An artist of astounding virtuosity had chosen to paint a close-up of natural objects seen in their own context and without reference to merely human notions of what's what, or what ought to be what. Man, we like to say, is the measure of all things. For

Monet, on this occasion, water lilies were the measure of water lilies; and so he painted them.

The same non-human point of view must be adopted by any artist who tries to render the distant scene. How tiny, in the Chinese painting, are the travellers who make their way along the valley! How frail the bamboo hut on the slope above them! And all the rest of the vast landscape is emptiness and silence. This revelation of the wilderness, living its own life according to the laws of its own being, transports the mind towards its antipodes; for primeval Nature bears a strange resemblance to that inner world where no account is taken of our personal wishes or even of the enduring concerns of man in general.

Only the middle distance and what may be called the remoter foreground are strictly human. When we look very near or very far, man either vanishes altogether or loses his primacy. The astronomer looks even further afield than the Sung painter and sees even less of human life. At the other end of the scale the physicist, the chemist, the physiologist pursue the close-up - the cellular close-up, the molecular, the atomic, and sub-atomic. Of that which, at twenty feet, even at arm's length, looked and sounded like a human being no trace remains.

Something analogous happens to the myopic artist and the happy lover. In the nuptial embrace personality is melted down; the individual (it is the recurrent theme of Lawrence's poems and novels) ceases to be himself and becomes a part of the vast impersonal universe.

And so it is with the artist who chooses to use his eyes at the near point. In his work humanity loses its importance, even disappears completely. Instead of men and women playing their fantastic tricks before high heaven, we are asked to consider the lilies, to meditate on the unearthly beauty of 'mere things', when isolated from their utilitarian context and rendered as they are, in and for themselves. Alternatively (or, at an earlier stage of artistic development, exclusively), the non-human world of the near-point is rendered in patterns. These patterns are abstracted for the most part from leaves and flowers - the rose, the lotus, the acanthus, palm, papyrus - and are elaborated, with recurrences and variations, into something transportingly reminiscent of the living geometries of the Other World.

Freer and more realistic treatments of Nature at the near-point make their appearance at a relatively recent date - but far earlier than those treatments of the distant scene, to which alone (and mistakenly) we give the name of landscape painting. Rome, for example, had its close-up landscapes. The fresco of a garden, which once adorned a room in Livia's villa, is a magnificent example of this form of art.

For theological reasons, Islam had to be content, for the most part, with 'arabesques' - luxuriant and (as in visions) continually varying patterns, based upon natural objects seen at the near-point. But even in Islam the genuine close-up landscape was not unknown. Nothing can exceed in beauty and in vision-inducing power the mosaics of gardens and buildings hi the great Omayyad mosque at Damascus.

In medieval Europe, despite the prevailing mania for turning every datum into a concept, every immediate experience into a mere symbol of something in a book, realistic close-ups of foliage and flowers were fairly common. We find them carved on the capitals of Gothic pillars, as in the Chapter House of Southwell Minster. We find them in paintings of the chase - paintings whose subject was that ever present fact of medieval life, the forest, seen as the hunter or the strayed traveller sees it, in all its bewildering intricacy of leafy detail.

The frescoes in the papal palace at Avignon are almost the sole survivors of what, even in the time of Chaucer, was a widely practised form of secular art. A century later this art of the forest close-up came to its self-conscious perfection in such magnificent and magical works as Pisanello's *St Hubert* and Paolo Uccello's *Hunt in a Wood*, now in the Ashmolean Museum at Oxford. Closely related to the wall paintings of forest close-ups were the tapestries, with which the rich men of northern Europe adorned their houses. The best of these are vision-inducing works of the highest order. In their own way they are as heavenly, as powerfully reminiscent of what goes on at the mind's antipodes, as are the great masterpieces of landscape painting at the furthest point - Sung mountains in their enormous solitude, Ming rivers interminably lovely, the blue sub-Alpine world of Titian's distances, the England of Constable; the Italics of Turner and Corot; the Provences of Cezanne and Van Gogh; the Ile de France of Sisley and the Ile de France of Vuillard.

Vuillard, incidentally, was a supreme master both of the transporting close-up and of the transporting distant view. His bourgeois interiors are masterpieces of vision-inducing art, compared with which the works of such conscious and so to say professional visionaries as Blake and Odilon Redon seem feeble in the extreme. In Vuillard's interiors every detail however trivial, however hideous even - the pattern of the late Victorian wallpaper, the Art Nouveau bibelot, the Brussels carpet - is seen and rendered as a living jewel; and all these jewels are harmoniously combined into a whole which is a jewel of a yet higher order of visionary intensity. And when the upper middle-class inhabitants of Vuillard's New Jerusalem go for a walk, they find themselves not, as they had supposed, in the department of Seine-et-Oise, but in the Garden of Eden, in an Other World which is yet essentially the same as this world, but transfigured and therefore transporting. (See App. V)

I have spoken so far only of the blissful visionary experience and of its interpretation in terms of theology, its translation into art. But visionary experience is not always blissful, It is sometimes terrible. There is hell as well as heaven.

Like heaven, the visionary hell has its praeternatural light and its praeternatural significance. But the significance is intrinsically appalling and the light is 'the smoky light' of the *Tibetan Book of the Dead*, the 'darkness visible' of Milton. In the *Journal d'une schizophrene* (M. A. Sechehaye. Paris, 1950), the autobiographical record of a young girl's passage through madness, the world of the schizophrenic is called *le pays d'eclairement* - 'the country of lit-upness'. It is a name which a mystic might have used to denote his heaven.

But for poor Renee, the schizophrenic, the illumination is infernal - an intense electric glare without a shadow, ubiquitous and implacable. Everything that, for healthy visionaries, is a source of bliss, brings to Renee only fear and a nightmarish sense of unreality. The summer sunshine is malignant; the gleam of polished surfaces is suggestive, not of gems, but of machinery and enamelled tin; the intensity of existence which animates every object, when seen at close range and out of its utilitarian context, is felt as a menace.

And then there is the horror of infinity. For the healthy visionary, the perception of the infinite in a finite particular is a revelation of divine immanence; for Renee, it was a revelation of what she calls 'the System', the vast cosmic mechanism which exists only to grind out guilt and punishment, solitude and unreality. (See App. VI.)

Sanity is a matter of degree, and there are plenty of visionaries who see the world as Renee saw it, but contrive, none the less, to live outside the asylum. For them, as for the positive visionary, the universe is transfigured - but for the worse. Everything in it, from the stars in the sky to the dust under their feet, is unspeakably sinister or disgusting; every event is charged with a hateful significance; every object manifests the presence of an Indwelling Horror, infinite, all-powerful, eternal.

This negatively transfigured world has found its way, from time to time, into literature and the arts. It writhed and threatened in Van Gogh's later landscapes; it was the setting and the theme of all Kafka's stories; it was Gericault's spiritual home (See App II); it was inhabited by Goya during the years of his deafness and solitude; it was glimpsed by Browning when he wrote Childe Roland; it had its place, over against the theophanies, in the novels of Charles Williams.

The negative visionary experience is often accompanied by bodily sensations of a very special and characteristic kind. Blissful visions are generally associated with a sense of separation from the body, a feeling of de-individualization. (It is, no doubt, this feeling of de-individualization which makes it possible for the Indians who practice the peyote cult to use the drug not merely as a short cut to the visionary world, but also as an instrument for creating a loving solidarity within the participating group.) When the visionary experience is terrible and the world is transfigured for the worse, individualization is intensified and the negative visionary finds himself associated with a body that seems to grow progessively more dense, more tightly packed, until he finds himself at last reduced to being the agonized consciousness of an inspissated lump of matter, no bigger than a stone that can be held between the hands.

It is worth remarking, that many of the punishments described in the various accounts of hell are punishments of pressure and constriction. Dante's sinners are buried in mud, shut up in the trunks of trees, frozen solid in blocks of ice, crushed beneath stones. The Inferno is psychologically true. Many of its pains are experienced by schizophrenics, and by those who have taken mescalin or lysergic acid under unfavourable conditions. (See App. VIII)

What is the nature of these unfavourable conditions? How and why is heaven turned into hell? In certain cases the negative visionary experience is the result of predominantly physical causes. Mescalin tends, after ingestion, to accumulate in the liver. If the liver is diseased, the associated mind may find itself in hell. But what is more important for our present purposes is the fact that negative visionary experience may be induced by purely psychological means. Fear and anger bar the way to the heavenly Other World and plunge the mescalin taker into hell.

And what is true of the mescalin taker is also true of the person who sees visions spontaneously or under hypnosis. Upon this psychological foundation has been reared the theological doctrine of saving faith - a doctrine to be met with in all the great religious traditions of the world. Eschatologists have always found it difficult to reconcile their rationality and their morality with the brute facts of psychological experience. As rationalists and moralists, they feel that good behaviour should be rewarded and that the virtuous deserve to go to heaven. But as psychologists they know that virtue is not the sole or sufficient condition of blissful visionary experience. They know that works alone are powerless and that it is faith, or loving confidence, which guarantees that visionary experience shall be blissful.

Negative emotions - the fear which is the absence of confidence, the hatred, anger, or malice which exclude love - are the guarantee that visionary experience, if and when it comes, shall be appalling. The Pharisee is a virtuous man; but his virtue is of the kind which is compatible with negative emotion. His visionary experiences are therefore likely to be infernal rather than blissful.

The nature of the mind is such that the sinner who repents and makes an act of faith in a higher power is more likely to have a blissful visionary experience than is the self-satisfied pillar of society with his righteous indignations, his anxiety about possessions and pretensions, his ingrained habits of blaming, despising, and condemning. Hence the enormous importance attached, in all the great religious traditions, to the state of mind at the moment of death.

Visionary experience is not the same as mystical experience. Mystical experience is beyond the realm of opposites. Visionary experience is still within that realm. Heaven entails hell, and 'going to heaven' is no more liberation than is the descent into horror. Heaven is merely a vantage point from which the divine Ground can be more clearly seen than on the level of ordinary individualized existence.

If consciousness survives bodily death, it survives, presumably, on every mental level - on the level of mystical experience, on the level of blissful visionary experience, on the level of infernal visionary experience, and on the level of everyday individual existence.

In life, even the blissful visionary experience tends to change its sign if it persists too long. Many schizophrenics have their times of heavenly happiness; but the fact that (unlike the mescalin taker) they do not know when, if ever, they will be permitted to return to the reassuring banality of everyday experience causes even heaven to seem appalling. But for those who, for whatever reason, are appalled, heaven turns into hell, bliss into horror, the Clear Light into the hateful glare of the land of lit-upness.

Something of the same kind may happen in the posthumous state. After having had a glimpse of the unbearable splendour of ultimate Reality, and after having shuttled back and forth between heaven and hell, most souls find it possible to retreat into that more reassuring region of the mind, where they can use their own and other people's wishes, memories, and fancies to construct a world very like that in which they lived on earth.

Of those who die an infinitesimal minority are capable of immediate union with the divine Ground, a few are capable of supporting the visionary bliss of heaven, a few find themselves in the visionary horrors of hell and are unable to escape; the great majority end up in the kind of world described by Swedenborg and the mediums. From this world it is doubtless possible to pass, when the necessary conditions have been fulfilled, to worlds of visionary bliss or the final enlightenment.

My own guess is that modern spiritualism and ancient tradition are both correct. There is a posthumous state of the kind described in Sir Oliver Lodge's book, Raymond; but there is also a heaven of blissful visionary experience; there is also a hell of the same kind of appalling visionary experience as is suffered here by schizophrenics and some of those who take mescalin; and there is also an experience, beyond time, of union with the divine Ground.

APPENDICES

APPENDIX I

Two other, less effective aids to visionary experience deserve mention - carbon dioxide and the stroboscopic lamp. A mixture (completely non-toxic) of seven parts of oxygen and three of carbon dioxide produces, in those who inhale it, certain physical and psychological changes, which have been exhaustively described by Meduna. Among these changes the most important, in our present context, is a marked enhancement of the ability to 'see things', when the eyes are closed. In some cases only swirls of patterned colour are seen. In others there may be vivid recalls of past experiences. (Hence the value of CO 2 as a therapeutic agent.) In yet other cases carbon dioxide transports the subject to the Other World at the antipodes of his everyday consciousness, and he enjoys very briefly visionary experiences entirely unconnected with his own personal history or with the problems of the human race in general.

In the light of these facts it becomes easy to understand the rationale of yogic breathing exercises. Practised systematically, these exercises result, after a time, in prolonged suspensions of breath. Long suspensions of breath lead to a high concentration of carbon dioxide in the lungs and blood, and this increase in the concentration of CO 2 lowers the efficiency of the brain as a reducing valve and permits the entry into consciousness of experiences, visionary or mystical, from 'out there'.

Prolonged and continuous shouting or singing may produce similar, but less strongly marked, results. Unless they are highly trained, singers tend to breathe out more than they breathe in. Consequently the concentration of carbon dioxide in the alveolar air and the blood is increased and, the efficiency of the cerebral reducing valve being lowered, visionary experience becomes possible. Hence the interminable 'vain repetitions' of magic and religion. The chanting of the curandero, the medicine-man, the shaman; the endless psalm-singing and sutra-intoning of Christian and Buddhist monks; the shouting and howling, hour after hour, of revivalists - under all the diversities of theological belief and aesthetic convention, the psychochemico-physiological intention remains constant. To increase the concentration of CO 2 in the lungs and blood and so to lower the efficiency of the cerebral reducing valve, until it will admit biologically useless material from Mind-at-Large - this, though the shouters, singers, and mutterers did not know it, has been at all times the real purpose and point of magic spells, of mantrams, litanies, psalms, and sutras. 'The heart,' said Pascal, 'has its reasons.' Still more cogent and much harder to unravel are the reasons of the lungs, the blood, and the enzymes, of neurones and synapses. The way to the super-conscious is through the subconscious, and the way, or at least one of the ways, to the subconscious is through the chemistry of individual cells.

With the stroboscopic lamp we descend from chemistry to the still more elementary realm of physics. Its rhythmically flashing light seems to act directly, through the optic nerves, on the electrical manifestations of the brain's activity. (For this reason there is always a slight danger involved in the use of the stroboscopic lamp. Some persons suffer from petit mal without being made aware of the fact by any clear-cut and unmistakable symptoms. Exposed to a stroboscopic lamp, such persons may go into a full-blown epileptic fit. The risk is not very great; but it must always be recognized. One case in eighty may turn out badly.)

To sit, with eyes closed, in front of a stroboscopic lamp is a very curious and fascinating experience. No sooner is the lamp turned on than the most brilliantly coloured patterns make themselves visible. These patterns are not static, but change incessantly. Their prevailing colour is a function of the stroboscope's rate of discharge. When the lamp is flashing at any speed between ten to fourteen or fifteen times a second, the patterns are prevailingly orange and red. Green and blue make their appearance when the rate exceeds fifteen flashes a second. After eighteen or nineteen, the patterns become white and grey. Precisely why we should see such patterns under the stroboscope is not known. The most obvious explanation would be in terms of the interference of two or more rhythms - the rhythm of the lamp and the various rhythms of the brain's electrical activity. Such interferences may be translated by the visual centre and optic nerves into something, of which the mind becomes conscious as a coloured, moving pattern. Far more difficult to explain is the fact, independently observed by several experimenters, that the stroboscope tends to enrich and intensify the visions induced by mescalin or lysergic acid. Here, for example, is a case communicated to me by a medical friend. He had taken lysergic acid and was seeing, with his eyes shut, only coloured, moving patterns. Then he sat down in front of a stroboscope. The lamp was turned on and, immediately, abstract geometry was transformed into what my friend described as 'Japanese land-scapes' of surpassing beauty. But how on earth can the interference of two rhythms produce an arrangement of electrical impulses interpretable as a living, self-modulating Japanese landscape unlike anything the subject has ever seen, suffused with praeternatural light and colour, and charged with praeter-natural significance?

This mystery is merely a particular case of a larger, more com-prehensive mystery - the nature of the relations between visionary experience and events on the cellular, chemical, and electrical levels. By touching certain areas of the brain with a very fine electrode, Penfield has been able to induce the recall of a long chain of memories relating to some past experience. This recall is not merely accurate on every perceptual detail; it is also accompanied by all the emotions which were aroused by the events when they originally occurred. The patient, who is under a local anaesthetic, finds himself simultaneously in two times and places - in the operating room, now, and in his childhood home, hundreds of miles away and thousands of days in the past. Is there, one wonders, some area in the brain from which the probing electrode could elicit Blake's Cherubim, or Weir Mitchell's self-transforming Gothic tower encrusted with living gems, or my friend's unspeak-ably lovely Japanese landscapes? And if, as I myself believe, vision-ary experiences enter our consciousness from somewhere 'out there' in the infinity of Mind-at-Large, what sort of an ad hoc neurological pattern is created for them by the receiving and transmitting brain? And what happens to this ad hoc pattern, when the vision is ' over? Why do all visionaries insist on the imposs-ibility of recalling, in anything even faintly resembling its original form and intensity, their transfiguring experiences? How many questions - and, as yet, how few answers!

APPENDIX II

In the Western world visionaries and mystics are a good deal less common than they used to be. There are two principal reasons for this state of affairs - a philosophical reason and a chemical reason. In the currently fashionable picture of the universe there is no place for valid transcendental experience. Consequently those who have had what they regard as valid transcendental experiences are looked upon with suspicion, as being either lunatics or swindlers. To be a mystic or a visionary is no longer creditable.

But it is not only our mental climate that is unfavourable to the visionary and the mystic; it is also our chemical environment - an environment profoundly different from that in which our forefathers passed their lives.

The brain is chemically controlled, and experience has shown that it can be made permeable to the (biologically speaking) superfluous aspects of Mind-at-Large by modifying the (biologically speaking) normal chemistry of the body.

For almost half of every year our ancestors ate no fruit, no green vegetables, and (since it was impossible for them to feed more than a few oxen, cows, swine, and poultry during the winter months) very little butter or fresh meat, and very few eggs. By the beginning of each successive spring, most of them were suffering, mildly or acutely, from scurvy, due to lack of vitamin C, and pellagra, caused by a shortage in their diet of the B complex. The distressing physical symptoms of these diseases are associated with no less distressing psychological symptoms. (See The Biology of Human Starvation, by A. Keys (University of Minnesota Press 1950); also the recent (1955) reports of .the work on the role of vitamin deficiencies in mental disease carried out by Dr George Watson and his associates in Southern California.

The nervous system is more vulnerable than the other tissues of the body; consequently vitamin deficiencies tend to affect the state of mind before they affect, at least in any very obvious way, the skin, bones, mucous membranes, muscles, and viscera. The first result of an inadequate diet is a lowering of the efficiency of the brain as an instrument for biological survival. The undernourished person tends to be afflicted by anxiety, depression, hypochondria, and feelings of anxiety. He is also liable to see visions; for when the cerebral reducing valve has its efficiency reduced, much (biologically speaking) useless material flows into consciousness from 'out there', in Mind-at-Large.

Much of what the earlier visionaries experienced was terrifying. To use the language of Christian theology, the Devil revealed himself in their visions and ecstasies a good deal more frequently than did God. In an age when vitamins were deficient and a belief in -Satan universal, this was not surprising. The mental distress, associated with even mild cases of pellagra and scurvy, was deepened by fears of damnation and a conviction that the powers of evil were omnipresent. This distress was apt to tinge with its own dark colouring the visionary material, admitted to consciousness through a cerebral valve whose efficiency had been impaired by underfeeding. But in spite of their preoccupations with eternal punishment and in spite of their deficiency disease, spiritually minded ascetics often saw heaven and might even be aware, occasionally, of that divinely impartial One, in which the polar opposites are reconciled. For a glimpse of beatitude, for a foretaste of unitive knowledge, no price seemed too high. Mortification of the body may produce a host of undesirable mental symptoms; but it may also open a door into a transcendental world of Being, Knowledge, and Bliss. That is why, in spite of its obvious disadvantages, almost all aspirants to the spiritual life have, in the past, undertaken regular courses of bodily mortification.

So far as vitamins were concerned, every medieval winter was a long involuntary fast, and this involuntary fast was followed, during Lent, by forty days of voluntary abstinence-Holy Week found the faithful marvellously well prepared, so far as their body chemistry was concerned, for its tremendous incitements to grief and joy, for seasonable remorse of conscience and a self-transcending identification with the risen Christ. At this season of the highest religious excitement and the lowest vitamin intake, ecstasies and visions were almost a commonplace. It was only to be expected.

For cloistered contemplatives, there were several Lents in every year. And even between fasts their diet was meagre in the extreme. Hence those agonies of depression and scrupulosity described by so many spiritual writers; hence their frightful temptations to despair and self-slaughter. But hence too those 'gratuitous graces', in the forms of heavenly visions and locutions, of prophetic insights, of telepathic 'discernments of spirits'. And hence, finally, their 'infused contemplation', their 'obscure knowledge' of the One in all.

Fasting was not the only form of physical mortification resorted to by the earlier aspirants to spirituality. Most of them regularly used upon themselves the whip of knotted leather or even of iron wire. These beatings were the equivalent of fairly extensive surgery without anaesthetics, and their effects on the body chemistry of the penitent were considerable. Large quantities of histamine and adrenalin were released while the whip was actually being plied; and when the resulting wounds began to fester (as wounds practically always did before the age of soap), various toxic substances, produced by the decomposition of protein, found their way into the bloodstream. But histamine produces shock, and shock affects the mind no less profoundly than the body. Moreover, large quantities of adrenalin may cause hallucinations, and some of the products of its decomposition are known to induce symptoms resembling those of schizophrenia. As for toxins from wounds - these upset the enzyme systems regulating the brain, and lower its efficiency as an instrument for getting on in a world where the biologically fittest survive. This may explain why the Cure d'Ars used to say that, in the days when he was free to flagellate himself without mercy, God would refuse him nothing. In other words, when remorse, self-loathing, and the fear of hell release adrenalin, when self-inflicted surgery releases adrenalin and histamine, and when infected wounds release decomposed protein into the blood, the efficiency of the cerebral reducing valve is lowered and unfamiliar aspects of Mind-at-Large (including psi phenomena, visions, and, if he is philosophically and ethically prepared for it, mystical experiences) will flow into the ascetic's consciousness.

Lent, as we have seen, followed a long period of involuntary fasting. Analogously, the effects of self-flagellation were supplemented, in earlier times, by much involuntary absorption of decomposed protein. Dentistry was non-existent, surgeons were executioners, and there were no safe antiseptics. Most people, therefore, must have lived out then-lives with focal infections; and focal infections, though out of fashion as the cause of all the ills that flesh is heir to, can certainly lower the efficiency of the cerebral reducing valve.

And the moral of all this is - what? Exponents of a Nothing-But philosophy will answer that, since changes in body chemistry can create the conditions favourable to visionary and mystical experience, visionary and mystical experience cannot be what they claim to be - what, for those who have had them, they self-evidently are. But this, of course, is a non sequitur.

A similar conclusion will be reached by those whose philosophy is unduly 'spiritual'. God, they will insist, is a spirit and is to be worshipped in spirit. Therefore an experience which is chemically conditioned cannot be an experience of the divine. But, in one way or another, all our experiences are chemically conditioned, and if we imagine that some of them are purely 'spiritual', purely 'intellectual', purely 'aesthetic', it is merely because we have never troubled to investigate the internal chemical environment at the moment of their occurrence. Furthermore, it is a matter of historical record that most contemplatives worked systematically to modify their body chemistry, with a view to creating the internal conditions favourable to spiritual insight. When they were not starving themselves into low blood sugar and a vitamin deficiency, or beating themselves into intoxication by histamine, adrenalin, and decomposed protein, they were cultivating insomnia and praying for long periods in uncomfortable positions, in order to create the psycho-physical symptoms of stress. In the intervals they sang interminable psalms, thus increasing the amount of carbon dioxide in the lungs and the blood-stream, or, if they were Orientals, they did breathing exercises to accomplish the same purpose. To-day we know how to lower the efficiency of the cerebral reducing valve by direct chemical action, and without die risk of inflicting serious damage on the psycho-physical organism. For an aspiring mystic to revert, in the present state of knowledge, to prolonged fasting and violent self-flagellation would be as senseless as it would be for an aspiring cook to behave like Charles Lamb's Chinaman, who burned down the house in order to roast a pig. Knowing as he does (or at least as he can know, if he so desires) what are the chemical conditions of transcendental experience, the aspiring mystic should turn for technical help to the specialists - in pharmacology, in bio-chemistry, in physiology and neurology, in psychology and psychiatry and parapsychology. And on their part, of course, the specialists (if any of them aspire to be genuine men of science and complete human beings) should turn, out of their respective pigeon-holes, to the artist, the sibyl, the visionary, the mystic - all those, in a word, who have had experience of the Other World and who know, in their different ways, what to do with that experience.

APPENDIX III

Vision-like effects and vision-inducing devices have played a greater part in popular entertainment than in the fine arts. Fireworks, pageantry, theatrical spectacle - these are essentially visionary arts. Unfortunately they are also ephemeral arts, whose earlier masterpieces are known to us only by report. Nothing remains of all the Roman triumphs, the medieval tournaments, the

Jacobean masques, the long succession of state entries and coronations, of royal marriages and solemn decapitations, of canonizations and the funerals of Popes. The best that can be hoped for such magnificences is that they may 'live in Settle's numbers one day more'.

An interesting feature of these popular visionary arts is their close dependence upon contemporary technology. Fireworks, for example, were once no more than bonfires (and to this day, I may add, a good bonfire on a dark night remains one of the most magical and transporting of spectacles. Looking at it, one can understand the mentality of the Mexican peasant, who sets out to burn an acre of woodland in order to plant his maize, but is delighted when, by a happy accident, a square mile or two goes up in bright, apocalyptic flame). True pyrotechny began (in Europe at least, if not in China) with the use of combustibles in sieges and naval battles. From war it passed, in due course, to entertainment. Imperial Rome had its firework displays, some of which, even in its decline, were elaborate in the extreme. Here is Claudian's description of the show put on by Manlius Theodoras in A.D. 399.

Mobile ponderibus descendat pegma reductis inque chori speciem spargentes ardua flammas scaena rotet varios, et fingat Mulciber orbis per tabulas impune vagos pictaeque citato ludant igne trabes, et non permissa morari fida per innocuas errent incendia turres.

"Let the counterweights be removed," Mr Platnauer translates with a straightforwardness of language that does less than justice to the syntactical extravagances of the original, "and let the mobile crane descend, lowering on to the lofty stage men who, wheeling chorus-wise, scatter flames. Let Vulcan forge balls of fire to roll innocuously across the boards. Let the flames appear to play about the sham beams of the scenery and a tame conflagration, never allowed to rest, wander among the untouched towers."

After the fall of Rome, pyrotechny became, once more, exclusively a military art. Its greatest triumph was the invention by Callinicus, about A.D. 650, of the famous Greek Fire - the secret weapon which enabled a dwindling Byzantine Empire to hold out for so long against its enemies.

During the Renaissance fireworks re-entered the world of popular entertainment. With every advance in the science of chemistry, they became more and more brilliant. By the middle of the nineteenth century pyrotechny had reached a peak of technical perfection and was capable of transporting vast multitudes of spectators towards the visionary antipodes of minds which, consciously, were respectable Methodist, Puseyites, Utilitarians, disciples of Mill or Marx, of Newman, or Bradlaugh, or Samuel Smiles. In the Piazza del Popolo, at Ranelagh and the Crystal Palace, on every Fourth and Fourteenth of July, the popular subconscious was reminded by the crimson glare of strontium, by copper blue and barium green and sodium yellow, of that Other World, down under, in the psychological equivalent of Australia. Pageantry is a visionary art which has been used, from time immemorial, as a political instrument. The gorgeous fancy dress worn by Kings, Popes, and their respective retainers, military and ecclesiastical, has a very practical purpose - to impress the lower classes with a lively sense of their masters' superhuman greatness. By means of fine clothes and solemn ceremonies, *de facto* domination is transformed into a rule not merely *dejure*, but positively, *de lure divino*. The crowns and tiaras, the assorted jewellery, the satins, silks, and velvets, the gaudy uniforms and vestments, the crosses and medals, the sword hilts and the croziers, the plumes in the cocked hats and their clerical equivalents, those huge feather fans which make every papal function look like a tableau from Aida - all these are vision-inducing properties, designed to make all too human gentlemen and ladies look like heroes, demigoddesses, and seraphs, and giving, in the process, a great deal of innocent pleasure to all concerned, actors and spectators alike.

In the course of the last two hundred years the technology of artificial lighting has made enormous progress, and this progress has contributed very greatly to the effectiveness of pageantry and the closely related art of theatrical spectacle. The first notable advance was made in the eighteenth century, with the introduction of moulded spermaceti candles in place of the older tallow dip and poured wax taper. Next came the invention of Argand's tubular wick, with an air supply on the inner as well as the outer surface of the flame. Glass chimneys speedily followed, and it became possible, for the first time in history, to burn oil with a bright and completely smokeless light. Coal gas was first employed as an illuminant in the early years of the nineteenth century, and in 1825 Thomas Drummond found a practical way of heating lime to incandescence by means of an oxygen-hydrogen or oxygen-coal-gas flame. Meanwhile parabolic reflectors for concentrating light into a narrow beam had come into use. (The first English lighthouse equipped with such a reflector was built in 1790.)

The influence on pageantry and theatrical spectacle of these inventions was profound. In earlier times civic and religious ceremonies could only take place during the day (and days were as often cloudy as fine), or by the light, after sunset, of smoky lamps and torches or the feeble twinkling of candles. Argand and Drummond, gas, limelight, and, forty years later, electricity made it possible to evoke, from the boundless chaos of night, rich island universes, in which the glitter of metal and gems, the sumptuous glow of velvets and brocades were intensified to the highest pitch of what may be called intrinsic significance. A recent example of ancient pageantry, raised by twentieth-century lighting to a higher magical power, was the coronation of Queen Elizabeth II. In the motion picture of the event, a ritual of transporting splendour was saved from the oblivion which, up till now, has always been the fate of such solemnities, and preserved it, blazing praeternaturally under the floodlights, for the delight of a vast contemporary and future audience.

Two distinct and separate arts are practised in the theatre-the human art of the drama, and the visionary, other-world art of spectacle. Elements of the two arts may be combined in a single evening's entertainment - the drama being interrupted (as so often happens in elaborate productions of Shakespeare) to permit the audience to enjoy a tableau vivant, in which the actors either remain still or, if they move, move only in a non-dramatic way, ceremonyially, processionally, or in a formal dance. Our concern here is not with drama; it is with theatrical spectacle, which is simply pageantry without its political or religious overtones.

In the minor visionary arts of the costumier and the designer of stage jewellery our ancestors were consummate masters. Nor, for all their dependence on unassisted muscle power, were they far behind us in the building and working of stage machinery, the contrivance of 'special effects'. In the masques of Elizabethan and early Stuart times, divine descents and irruptions of demons from the cellarage were a commonplace; so were apocalypses, so were the most amazing metamorphoses. Enormous sums of money were lavished on these spectacles. The Inns of Court, for example, put on a show for Charles I which cost more than twenty thousand pounds - at a date when the purchasing power of the pound was six or seven times what it is to-day.

'Carpentry,' said Ben Jonson sarcastically, 'is the soul of masque.' His contempt was motivated by resentment. Inigo Jones was paid as much for designing the scenery as was Ben for writing the libretto. The outraged laureate had evidently failed to grasp the fact that masque is a visionary art, and that visionary experience is beyond words (at any rate beyond all but the most Shakespearean words) and is to be evoked by direct, unmediated perceptions of things that remind the beholder of what is going on at the unexplored antipodes of his own personal consciousness. The soul of masque could never, in the very nature of things, be a Jonsonian libretto; it had to be carpentry. But even carpentry could not be the masque's whole soul. When it comes to us from within, visionary experience is always praeternaturally brilliant. But the early set designers possessed no manageable illuminant brighter than a candle. At close range a candle can create the most magical lights and contrasting shadows. The visionary paintings of Rembrandt and Georges dc La Tour are of things and persons seen by candlelight. Unfortunately light obeys the law of the inverse squares. At a safe distance from an actor in inflammable fancy dress, candles are hopelessly inadequate. At ten feet, for example, it would take one hundred of the best wax tapers to produce an effective illumination of one foot-candle. With such miserable lighting only a fraction of the masque's visionary potentialities could be made actual. Indeed, its visionary potentialities were not fully realized until long after it had ceased, in its original form, to exist. It was only in the nineteenth century, when advancing technology had equipped the theatre with limelight and parabolic reflectors, that the masque came fully into its own. Victoria's reign was the heroic age of the so-called Christmas pantomime and the fantastic spectacle. 'Ali Baba', 'The King of the Peacocks', 'The Golden Branch', 'The Island of Jewels' - their very names are magical. The soul of that theatrical magic was carpentry and dressmaking; its indwelling spirit, its *scintilla animae*, was gas and limelight and, after the eighties, electricity. For the first time in the history of the stage, beams of brightest incandescence transfigured the painted backdrops, the costumes, the glass and pinch-beck of jewellery, so that they became capable of transporting the spectators towards that Other World which lies at the back of every mind, however perfect its adaptation to the exigencies of social life - even the social life of Mid-Victorian England. To-day we are in the fortunate position of being able to squander half a million horsepower on the nightly illumination of a metropolis. And yet, in spite of this devaluation of artificial light, theatrical spectacle still retains its old compelling magic. Embodied in ballets, revues, and musical comedies, the soul of masque goes marching along. Thousand-watt lamps and parabolic reflectors project beams of praeternatural light, and praeternatural light evokes, in everything it touches, praeternatural colour and praeternatural significance. Even the silliest spectacle can be rather wonderful. It is a case of a New World having been called in to redress the balance of the Old - of visionary art making up for the deficiencies of all-too-human drama.

Athanasius Kircher's invention - if his, indeed, it was - was Christened from the first Lanterna Magica. The name was everywhere adopted as perfectly appropriate to a machine, whose raw material was light, and whose finished product was a coloured image emerging from the darkness. To make the original magic lantern show yet more magical, Kircher's successors devised a number of methods for imparting life and movement to the projected image. There were 'chroma-tropic' slides, in which two painted glass discs could be made to revolve in opposite directions, producing a crude but still effective imitation of those perpetually changing three-dimensional patterns, which have been seen by virtually everyone who has had a vision, whether spontaneous or induced by drugs, fasting, or the stroboscopic lamp. Then there were those 'dissolving views', which reminded the spectator of the metamorphoses going on incessantly at the antipodes of his everyday consciousness. To make one scene turn imperceptibly into another, two magic lanterns were used, projecting coincident images on the screen. Each lantern was fitted with a shutter, so arranged that the light of one could be progressively dimmed, while the light of the other (originally completely obscured) was progressively brightened. In this way the view projected by the first lantern was insensibly replaced by the view by the second - to the delight and astonishment of all beholders. Another device was the mobile magic lantern, projecting its image on a semi-transparent screen, on the further side of which sat the audience. When the lantern was wheeled close to the screen, the projected image was very small. As it was withdrawn, the image became progressively larger. An automatic focusing device kept the changing images sharp and unblurred at all distances. The word 'phantasmagoria' was coined in 1802 by the inventors of this new kind of peep-show.

All these improvements in the technology of magic lanterns were contemporary with the poets and painters of the Romantic Revival, and may perhaps have exercised a certain influence on their choice of subject-matter and their methods of treating it. *Queen Mab* and *The Revolt of Islam*, for example, are full of Dissolving Views and Phantasmagorias. Keats' descriptions of scenes and persons, of interiors and furniture and effects of light, have the intense beamy quality of coloured images on a white sheet in a darkened room. John Martin's representations of Satan and Belshazzar, of Hell and Babylon and the Deluge, are manifestly inspired by lantern slides and tableaux vivants dramatically illuminated by limelight.

The twentieth-century equivalent of the magic lantern show is the coloured movie. In the huge, expensive 'spectaculars', the soul of masque goes marching along - with a vengeance sometimes, but sometimes also with taste and a real feeling for vision-inducing phantasy. Moreover, thanks to advancing technology, the coloured documentary has proved itself, in skilful hands, a notable new form of popular visionary art. The immensely magnified cactus blossoms, into which, at the end of Disney's The Living Desert, the spectator finds himself sinking, come straight from the Other World. And then what transporting visions, in the best of the nature films, of foliage in the wind, of the textures of rock and sand, of the shadows and emerald lights in grass or among the reeds, of birds and insects and four-footed creatures going about their business in the underbrush or among the branches of forest trees! Here are the magical close-up landscapes which fascinated the makers of *millefeuilles* tapestries, the medieval painters of gardens and hunting scenes. Here are the enlarged and isolated details of living nature out of which the artists of the Far East made some of the most beautiful of their paintings.

And then there is what may be called the Distorted Documentary - a strange new form of visionary art, admirably exemplified by Mr Francis Thompson's film, 'NY, NY'. In this very strange and beautiful picture we see the city of New York as it appears when photographed through multiplying prisms, or reflected in the backs of spoons, polished hub caps, spherical and parabolic mirrors. We still recognize houses, people, shop fronts, taxi cabs, but recognize them as elements in one of those living geometries which are so characteristic of the visionary experience. The invention of this new cinematographic art seems to presage (thank heaven!) the supersession and early demise of non-representational painting. It used to be said by the non-representationalists that coloured photography had reduced the old-fashioned portrait and the old-fashioned landscape to the rank of otiose absurdities. This, of course, is completely untrue. Coloured photography merely records and preserves, in an easily reproducible form, the raw materials with which portraitists and landscape painters work. Used as Mr Thompson has used it, coloured cinematography does much more than merely record and preserve the raw materials of non-representational art; it actually turns out the finished product. Looking at 'NY, NY', I was amazed to see that virtually every pictorial device invented by the Old Masters of non-representational art and reproduced ad nauseam by the academicians and mannerists of the school, for the last forty years or more, makes its appearance, alive, glowing, intensely significant, in the sequences of Mr Thompson's film.

Our ability to project a powerful beam of light has not only enabled us to create new forms of visionary art; it has also endowed one of the most ancient arts, the art of sculpture, with a new visionary quality which it did not previously possess. I have spoken in an earlier paragraph of the magical effects produced by the floodlighting of ancient monuments and natural objects. Analogous effects are seen when we turn the spotlights on to sculptured stone. Fuseli got the inspiration for some of his best and wildest pictorial ideas by studying the statues on Monte Cavallo by the light of the setting sun, or, better still, when illuminated by lightning flashes at midnight. Today we dispose of artificial sunsets and synthetic lightning. We can illuminate our statues from whatever angle we choose, and with practically any desired degree of intensity. Sculpture, in consequence, has revealed fresh meanings and unsuspected beauties. Visit the Louvre one night, when the Greek and Egyptian antiquities are floodlit. You will meet with new gods, nymphs, and Pharaohs, you will make the acquaintance, as one spotlight goes out and another, in a different quarter of space, is lit up, of a whole family of unfamiliar Victories of Samothrace.

The past is not something fixed and unalterable. Its facts are rediscovered by every succeeding generation, its values re-assessed, its meanings re-defined in the context of present tastes and preoccupations. Out of the same documents and monuments and works of art, every epoch invents its own Middle Ages, its private

84

China, its patented and copyrighted Hellas. Today, thanks to recent advances in the technology of lighting, we can go one further than our predecessors. Not only have we reinterpreted the great works of sculpture bequeathed to us by the past; we have actually succeeded in altering the physical appearance of these works. Greek statues, as we see them illuminated by a light that never was on land or sea, and then photographed in a series of fragmentary close-ups from the oddest angles, bear almost no resemblance to the Greek statues seen by art critics and the general public in the dim galleries and decorous engravings of the past. The aim of the classical artist, in whatever period he may happen to live, is to impart order to the chaos of experience, to present a comprehensible, rational picture of reality in which all the parts are clearly seen and coherently related, so that the beholder knows (or, to be more accurate, imagines that he knows) precisely what's what. To us this ideal of rational orderliness makes no appeal. Consequently, when we are confronted by works of classical art, we use all the means in our power to make them look like something which they are not, and were never meant to be. From a work, whose whole point is its unity of conception, we select a single feature, focus our searchlights upon it, and so force it, out of all context, upon the observer's consciousness-Where a contour seems to us too continuous, too obviously comprehensible, we break it up by alternating impenetrable shadows with patches of glaring brightness. When we photograph a sculptured figure or group, we use the camera to isolate a part which we then exhibit in enigmatic independence from the whole. By such means we can de-classicize the severest classic. Subjected to the light treatment and photographed by an expert camera man, a Pheidias becomes a piece of Gothic expressionism, a Praxiteles is turned into a fascinating surrealiste object dredged up from the ooziest depths of the subconscious. This may be bad art history, but it is certainly enormous fun.

APPENDIX IV

Painter in ordinary first to the Duke of his native Lorraine and later to the King of France, Georges de La Tour was treated, during his lifetime, as the great artist he so manifestly was. With the accession of Louis XIV and the rise, the deliberate cultivation, of a new Art of Versailles, aristocratic in subject-matter and lucidly classical in style, the reputation of this once famous man suffered an eclipse so complete that, within a couple of generations, his very name had been forgotten, and his surviving paintings came to be attributed to the Le Nains, to Honthorst, to Zurbaran, to Murillo, even to Velasquez. The rediscovery of La Tour began in 1915 and was virtually complete by 1934, when the Louvre organized a notable exhibition of 'The Painters of Reality'. Ignored for nearly three hundred years, one of the greatest of French painters had come back to claim his rights.

Georges de La Tour was one of those extroverted visionaries, whose art faithfully reflects certain aspects of the outer world, but reflects them in a state of transfigurement, so that every meanest particular becomes intrinsically significant, a manifestation of the absolute. Most of his compositions are of figures seen by the light of a single candle. A single candle, as Caravaggio and the Spaniards had shown, can give rise to the most enormous theatrical effects. But La Tour took no interest in theatrical effects. There is nothing dramatic in his pictures, nothing tragic or pathetic or grotesque, no representation of action, no appeal to the sort of emotions which people go to the theatre to have excited and then appeased. His personages are essentially static. They never do anything; they are simply there in the same way in which a granite Pharaoh is there, or a Bodhisattva from Khmer, or one of Piero's flat-footed angels. And the single candle is used, in every case, to stress this intense but unexcited, impersonal thereness. By exhibiting common things in an uncommon light, its flame makes manifest the living mystery and inexplicable marvel of mere existence. There is so little religiosity in the paintings that in many cases it is impossible to decide whether we are confronted by an illustration to the Bible or a study of models by candlelight. Is the 'Nativity' at Rennes the nativity, or merely a nativity? Is the picture of an old man asleep under the eyes of a young girl merely that? Or is it of St Peter in prison being visited by the delivering angel? There is no way of telling. But though La Tour's art is wholly without religiosity, it remains profoundly religious, in the sense that it reveals, with unexampled intensity, the divine omnipresence.

It must be added that, as a man, this great painter of God's immanence seems to have been proud, hard, intolerably overbearing, and avaricious. Which goes to show, yet once more, that there is never a one-to-one correspondence between an artist's work and his character.

APPENDIX V

At the near-point Vuillard painted interiors for the most part, but sometimes also gardens. In a few compositions he managed to combine the magic of propinquity with the magic of remoteness by representing a corner of a room, in which there stands or hangs one of his own, or someone else's, representation of a distant view of trees, hills, and sky. It is an invitation to make the best of both worlds, the telescopic and the microscopic, at a single glance.

For the rest, I can think of only a very few close-up landscapes by modern European artists. There is a strange *Thicket* by Van Gogh at the Metropolitan. There is Constable's wonderful *Dell in Helmingham Park* at the Tate. There is a bad picture, Millais' Ophelia, made magical, in spite of everything, by its intricacies of summer greenery seen from the point of view, very nearly, of a water rat. And I remember a Delacroix, glimpsed long ago at some Loan Exhibition, of bark and leaves and blossom at the closest range. There must, of course, be others; but either I have forgotten, or have never seen them. In any case there is nothing in the West comparable to the Chinese and Japanese renderings of nature at the near-point. A spray of blossoming plum, eighteen inches of a bamboo stem with its leaves, tits or finches seen at hardly more than arm's length among the bushes, all kinds of flowers and foliage, of birds and fish and small mammals. Each small life is represented as the centre of its own universe, the purpose, in its own estimation, for which this world and all that is in it were created; each issues its own specific and individual declaration of independence from human imperialism; each, by ironic impli-cation, derides our absurd pretensions to lay down merely human rules for the conduct of the cosmic game; each mutely repeats the divine tautology: I am that I am.

Nature at the middle distance is familiar - so familiar that we are deluded into believing that we really know what it is all about. Seen very close at hand, or at a great distance, or from an odd angle, it seems disquietingly strange, wonderful beyond all comprehension. The close-up landscapes of China and Japan are so many illustrations of the theme that Samsara and Nirvana are one, that the Absolute is manifest in every appearance. These great metaphysical, and yet pragmatic, truths were rendered by the Zen-inspired artists of the Far East in yet another way. All the objects of their near-point scrutiny were represented in a state of unrelated-ness, against a blank of virgin silk or paper. Thus isolated, these transient appearances take on a kind of absolute Thing-in-Itself-hood. Western artists have used this device when painting sacred figures, portraits, and, sometimes, natural objects at a distance. Rembrandt's *Mill* and Van Gogh's *Cypresses* are examples of long-range landscapes, in which a single feature has been absolutized by isolation. The magical power of many of Goya's etchings, draw-ings, and paintings can be accounted for by the fact that his com-positions almost always take the form of a few silhouettes, or even a single silhouette, seen against a blank. These silhouetted shapes possess the visionary quality of intrinsic significance, heightened by isolation and unrelatedness to praeternatural intensity.

In nature, as in a work of art, the isolation of an object tends to invest it with absoluteness, to endow it with that more-than-symbolic meaning which is identical with being.

But there's a tree - of many, *one* -
A *single* field which I have looked upon:
Both of them speak of something that is gone.

The something which Wordsworth could no longer see was 'the visionary gleam'. That gleam, I remember, and that intrinsic sig-nificance were the properties of a solitary oak that could be seen from the train, between Reading and Oxford, growing from the summit of a little knoll in a wide expanse of ploughland, and sil-houetted against the pale northern sky.

The effects of isolation combined with proximity may be stud-ied, in all their magical strangeness, in an extraordinary painting by a seventeenth-century Japanese artist, who was also a famous swordsman and a student of Zen. It represents a butcher bird, perched on the very tip of a naked branch, 'waiting without pur-pose, but in the state of highest tension'. Beneath, above, and all around is nothing. The bird emerges from the Void, from that eternal namelessness and formlessness, which is yet the very sub-stance of the manifold, concrete, and transient universe. That shrike on its bare branch is first cousin to Hardy's wintry thrush. But whereas the Victorian thrush insists on teaching us some kind of a lesson, the Far Eastern butcher-bird is content simply to exist, to be intensely and absolutely there.

APPENDIX VI

Many schizophrenics pass most of their time neither on earth, nor in heaven, nor even in hell, but in a grey, shadowy world of phantoms and unrealities. What is true of these psychotics is true, to a lesser extent, of certain neurotics afflicted by a milder form of mental illness. Recently it has been found possible to induce this state of ghostly existence by administering a small quantity of one of the derivatives of adrenalin. For the living, the doors of heaven, hell, and limbo are opened, not by 'massy keys of metals twain', but by the presence in the blood of one set of chemical compounds and the absence of another set. The shadow-world inhabited by some schizophrenics and neurotics closely resembles the world of the dead, as described in some of the earlier religious traditions. Like the wraiths in Sheol and in Homer's Hades, these mentally disturbed persons have lost touch with matter, language, and their fellow beings. They have no purchase on life and are condemned to ineffectiveness, solitude, and a silence broken only by the senseless squeak and gibber of ghosts.

The history of eschatological ideas marks a genuine progress - a progress which can be described in theological terms as the passage from Hades to Heaven, in chemical terms as the substitution of mescalin and lysergic acid for adrenolutin, and in psychological terms as the advance from catatonia and feelings of unreality to a sense of heightened reality in vision and, finally, in mystical experience.

APPENDIX VII

Gericault was a negative visionary; for though his art was almost obsessively true to nature, it was true to a nature that had been magically transfigured, in his perceiving and rendering of it, for the worse. 'I start to paint a woman,' he once said, 'but it always ends up as a lion.' More often, indeed it ended up as something a good deal less amiable than a lion - as a corpse, for example, or as a demon. His masterpiece, the prodigious *Raft of the Medusa*, was painted not from life but from dissolution and decay - from bits of cadavers supplied by medical students, from the emaciated torso and jaundiced face of a friend who was suffering from a disease of the liver. Even the waves on which the raft is floating, even the overarching sky are corpse-coloured. It is as though the entire universe had become a dissecting room.

And then there are his demonic pictures. *The Derby*, it is obvious, is being run in hell, against a background fairly blazing with darkness visible. 'The Horse startled by Lightning', in the National Gallery, is the revelation, in a single frozen instant, of the strangeness, the sinister, and even infernal otherness that hides in familiar things. In the Metropolitan Museum there is a portrait of a child. And what a child! In his luridly brilliant jacket the little darling is what Baudelaire liked to call 'a budding Satan', *un Satan en herbe*. And the study of a naked man, also in the Metropolitan, is none other than the budding Satan grown up.

From the accounts which his friends have left of him it is evident that Gericault habitually saw the world about him as a succession of visionary apocalypses. The prancing horse of his early *Officier de Chasseurs* was seen one morning, on the road to Saint-Cloud, in a dusty glare of summer sunshine, rearing and plunging between the shafts of an ombibus. The personages in the *Raft of the Medusa* were painted in finished detail, one by one, on the virgin canvas. There was no outline drawing of the whole composition, no gradual building up of an overall harmony of tones and hues. Each particular revelation - of a body in decay, of a sick man in the ghastly extremity of hepatitis - was fully rendered as it was seen and artistically realized. By a miracle of genius, every successive apocalypse was made to fit, prophetically, into a harmonious composition which existed, when the first of the appalling visions was transferred to canvas, only in the artist's imagination.

APPENDIX VIII

In *Sartor Resartus* Carlyle has left what (*in Mr Carlyle, my Patient*) his psychosomatic biographer, Dr James Halliday, calls 'an amazing description of a psychotic state of mind, largely depressive, but partly schizophrenic".

'The men and women around me,' writes Carlyle, 'even speaking with me, were but Figures; I had practically forgotten that they were alive, that they were not merely automata. Friendship was but an incredible tradition. In the midst of their crowded streets and assemblages I walked solitary; and (except that it was my own heart, not another's, that I kept devouring) savage also as the tiger in the jungle ... To me the Universe was all void of Life, of Purpose, of Volition, even of Hostility; it was one huge, dead immeasurable steam-engine, rolling on in its dead indifference, to grind me limb from limb ... Having no hope, neither had I any definite fear, were it of Man or of Devil. And yet, strangely enough, I lived in a continual, indefinite, pining fear, tremulous, pusil-lanimous, apprehensive of I knew not what; it seemed as if all things in the Heavens above and the Earth beneath, would hurt me; as if the Heavens and the Earth were but the boundless jaws of a devouring Monster, wherein I, palpitating, waited to be devoured.' Renee and the idolater of heroes are evidently describing the same experience. Infinity is apprehended by both, but in the form of 'the System', the 'immeasurable Steam-Engine'. To both, again, all is significant, but negatively significant, so that every event is utterly pointless, every object intensely unreal, every self-styled human being a clockwork dummy, grotesquely going through the motions of work and play, of loving, hating, thinking, of being eloquent, heroic, saintly, what you will - the robots are nothing if not ver-satile.

Also Available In

thINKing

SUCCESS CLASSICS

The Master Key System – *Charles F. Haanel*	978-1-907590-02-3
The Science Of Getting Rich – *Wallace D. Wattles*	978-1-907590-03-0
Think And Grow Rich – *Napoleon Hill*	978-1-907590-04-7
Thoughts Are Things – *Prentice Mulford*	978-1-907590-05-4
The Magic of Believing – *Claude M. Bristol*	978-1-907590-06-1

PROSPERITY CLASSICS

The Richest Man In Babylon – *George S. Clason*	978-1-907590-12-2
A Technique For Producing Ideas - *James W. Young*	978-1-907590-13-9
As A Man Thinketh – *James Allen*	978-1-907590-16-0
The Game of Life & How to Play It - *F Scovel-Shinn*	978-1-907590-14-6
The Secret Of The Ages – *Robert Collier*	978-1-907590-15-3

SPIRITUAL CLASSICS

The Prophet – *Kahlil Gibran*	978-1-907590-07-8
Siddhartha – *Hermann Hesse*	978-1-907590-08-5
The Doors of Perception – *Aldous Huxley*	978-1-907590-09-2
The Everlasting Man – *G. K. Chesterton*	978-1-907590-11-5
The Razor's Edge – *W. Somerset Maugham*	978-1-907590-10-8

POLITICAL CLASSICS

The Art Of War – *Sun Tzu*	978-1-907590-21-4
Utopia – *Thomas More*	978-1-907590-19-1
The Communist Manifesto – *Marx & Engels*	978-1-907590-17-7
The Social Contract – *Jean-Jacques Rousseau*	978-1-907590-20-7
The Prince – *Nicolo Machiavelli*	978-1-907590-18-4

www.thinkinginkmedia.com

CPSIA information can be obtained at www.ICGtesting.com
Printed in the USA
BVOW040926230512

290890BV00001B/96/P